# THE PRESENT AND FUTURE OF THE BASIS OF UNION

Fifty years on, the people of God 'on the way towards a promised goal' is a more diverse band, shaped by contemporary issues of identity, context and culture. Who are 'we' now, and what are the important signposts to navigate this journey? In this very welcome volume, a newer generation of pilgrims brings fresh insights to these questions, showing the enduring significance and ongoing interpretation of the *Basis of Union*.

Rev. Professor Vicky Balabanski
Principal
Uniting College for Leadership & Theology
Yarthu Apinthi
Kaurna Country

This collection of essays and reflections demonstrates that, fifty years on, the *Basis of Union* still has wisdom for the Church particularly when it is read with a loving but critical eye. The diversity of authors, the range of contexts and the fresh perspectives will help us read the *Basis of Union* in new ways and find new encouragement to continue the journey of uniting.

Sharon Hollis,
President, Uniting Church in Australia.
Narrm, Wurundjeri Country

The *Basis of Union* at 50 is an indispensable companion to the Uniting Church's visionary – and contested – founding document, and a welcome resource for all who seek faithful living in the tensions between tradition and innovation. The carefully curated collection navigates an appreciation for the *Basis* alongside astute and challenging interrogations of its silences, omissions and failures.

From the Indigenous perspectives of the opening chapters, recognising the complete omission of First Nations material from the *Basis*, to engagements from diverse other cultures who have, since colonisation, called these lands home, readers will be enriched and challenged. The reflections on the last 50 years provide an opportunity to consider what might be learned from the imperfections and gifts of the Basis' claims and our use of it.

This collection's insistent call not simply for including marginal voices, but recognising the theological primacy of the marginal should ground the conversation about the shape of any future guiding document and fire our imaginations about the place of tradition in the fresh words and deeds to which we are called.

Rev. Assoc. Professor Kylie Crabbe
Associate Professor of Biblical and Early Christian Studies
Australian Catholic University

MARKING FIFTY YEARS

# THE PRESENT
# AND FUTURE OF THE
# BASIS OF UNION

EDITORS

GEOFF THOMPSON & JI ZHANG

UAP

Uniting Academic Press
Melbourne

Published in Australia by
Uniting Academic Press
an imprint of Coventry Press
33 Scoresby Road
Bayswater VIC 3153

ISBN 9781922589422

Catalogue-in-Publication entry is available from the National Library of Australia
http://catalogue.nla.gov.au

Cover design by Ian James – www.jgd.com.au
Text design by Coventry Press
Set in EB Garamond

Printed in Australia

# Table of Contents

# Acknowledgments

Without the online conference at which most of the papers that follow were presented, this volume would not have emerged. Accordingly, our first acknowledgments must be paid to the various institutions and people who made the conference possible. Pilgrim Theological College sponsored, promoted and hosted the online conference. Our thanks, therefore, go to the Head of College, Rev Associate Professor Sean Winter, and the Faculty for this support. This included the technical assistance of Pilgrim's eLearning Co-ordinator, Adrian Jackson, in overseeing the technical demands of hosting an online conference. Also the assistance of the Hospitality Team at the Centre for Theology and Ministry was made available for the registration processes and for overseeing the pre-conference communications with over 80 presenters and participants.

The President of the Uniting Church Assembly, Rev Sharon Hollis, gave the conference her enthusiastic support and also chaired the day's proceedings. Of course, a special acknowledgment goes to all the presenters – both local and international – for the time and energy they gave to their reflection on the *Basis*. All these people helped to make the conference the success that it was.

Finally, the assistance of Pilgrim Theological College in providing financial support for the editorial work that led to this volume is also gratefully acknowledged. Of course, we are also grateful to Uniting Academic Press for accepting the book for publication and, in particular, Professor Katharine Massam and Hugh McGinlay, for their support

# Abbreviations

| | |
|---|---|
| BOU | *Basis of Union* (1992 edition). Available at "Basis of Union," *Uniting Church in Australia Assembly*, https://assembly.uca.org.au/basis-of-union References to paragraphs in the *Basis* are denoted as BOU, 1 etc |
| JCCU | Joint Commission on Church Union |
| FOTC | "The Faith of the Church," in *TFP*, 10-64. |
| CNFO | "The Church: Its Nature, Function and Ordering," in *TFP*, 69-186 |
| TFP | Bos, Rob and Geoff Thompson, *Theology for Pilgrims: Selected Theological Documents of t he Uniting Church* (Sydney: Uniting Church Press, 2008). |
| RevPreamble | "The Revised Preamble." Available at "The Revised Preamble," *Uniting Church in Australia Assembly*, https://assembly.uca.org.au/hef/item/668-the-revised-preamble |
| TCS | "The Covenanting Statement." Available at "Covenanting Statement," *Uniting Church in Australia, Resources* https://ucaassembly.recollect.net.au/nodes/view/310 |
| WAAMC | "We are a Multicultural Church." Available at *Uniting Church in Australia Assembly: Resources*, https://ucaassembly.recollect.net.au/nodes/view/494 |
| Assembly Minute | Reference to Assembly Minutes will be in the standard format: Year, Minute no, e.g. 18.03.01 |

indicates Minute 03.01 from the 2018 meeting of the Assembly. Full minutes can be accessed at *Uniting Church in Australia: Resources*, https://ucaassembly.recollect.net.au/nodes/browse/?meta=eyIxIjpbIk1pbnV0ZXMiXSwiMzIiOlsiTWlud XRlcyJ dLCIyOCI6WyJNaW51dGVzIl19

## The front cover image

The image on the front cover is of the final page of the original 1971 *Basis of Union* as approved by the Joint Commission on Church Union at its meeting in November 1970. It was formally designated the 1971 version in order to distinguish it from a version published earlier in 1970 but which was superseded by a small number or revisions approved at the November meeting. It was not published for public distribution until 1971. The signatures are those of members of the Joint Commission which were added at a later meeting (on an unknown date). The image is reproduced with the permission of the Uniting Church Assembly Archivist, Christine Gordon. The editors are grateful for Christine's assistance in tracking it down and making it available.

# Introduction

Geoff Thompson and Ji Zhang

This book emerged from an online conference hosted by Pilgrim Theological College on the 27th November 2021 to mark the 50th anniversary of the publication of the *Basis of Union* in 1971. The *Basis* was the document presented to the Congregational, Presbyterian and Methodist Churches to determine if they would unite to form the Uniting Church in Australia. After several years of debating, discernment and voting, it was accepted, thus enabling the formal inauguration of the Uniting Church on June 22nd 1977.

Over the years since union, the *Basis* has been invoked, interpreted, studied, criticised and championed. It has been in the background (and often the foreground) of many of the Uniting Church's significant debates about, for instance, baptism, women's ordination, ministry, and sexuality. It has also been revised: in 1992 an inclusive language version was published. That version is now established as the default version used in the life of the Uniting Church and the one referred to and quoted in this volume.

In the late 1990s, there was a sustained discussion about the continuing status and function of the *Basis*. Against an emerging view that it had exhausted its work in helping to bring the Uniting Church into being, the Assembly decided that, in fact, the *Basis* had the ongoing function of "guiding" the Church.[1] Academic discussion of the *Basis* during the first three decades of the church's

---

1  For an account of these discussions see Rob Bos, "The Revolting Fathers: the 1988 protest by the Basis of Union's framers," *Uniting Church Studies* 9, no. 1 (2003): 49-64.

life was, however, limited and somewhat spasmodic.[2] Then in the second decade of the 21st century, two academically-oriented conferences on the document were held, initially following the promptings of a meeting of the National Theological Educators' Consultation.

The first was held at the Centre for Theology and Ministry in Melbourne in 2010 and the second at Centre for Ministry in Sydney in 2014.[3] Both conferences were supported by the National Assembly through the involvement of the Assembly's then Consultant on Christian Unity, Doctrine and Worship, the Rev Dr Chris Walker. The second was specifically a project of the then Working Group on Doctrine and also had the support of Uniting World which had enabled the participation of two theologians from the China Christian Council. Notwithstanding

---

2  These contributions include: Andrew Dutney, *Manifesto for Renewal: The Shaping of a New Church* (Melbourne: Uniting Church Press, 1986); Michael Owen, *Back to Basics: Studies on the Basis of Union of the Uniting Church in Australia* (Collingwood: JBCE, 1996); Chris Budden, "Questioning the Basis," *Uniting Church Studies* 66, no. 2 (2000): 55-64; Andrew Dutney, *Where did the joy come from? Revisiting the Basis of Union* (Melbourne: Uniting Church Press, 2001); Howard Wallace, "Deuteronomy, the Basis of Union and an Act of Imagination," *Uniting Church Studies* 7, no 2 (2001):1-10; and Peter Walker, "Bonhoeffer and the Basis of Union," *Uniting Church Studies* 13, no. 1 (2007): 1-17.

3  A number of the papers presented at these conferences and some others on the *Basis* were later published in *Uniting Church Studies*. These include: Christiaan Mostert, "Christology in the Uniting Church in Australia," *Uniting Church Studies* 16, no 2 (2010): 33-42; Geoff Thompson, "'Well that's just your perspective': Guarding and Declaring the Right Understanding of the Faith in a Relativist Culture," *Uniting Church Studies* 17, no 2 (2011): 19-32; Benjamin Myers, "The Aesthetics of Christian Mission: New Creation and Mission in the Basis of Union," *Uniting Church Studies* 17, no 2 (2011): 45-54; Vicky Balabanski, "The Biblical Fabric of Paragraph 3 of the Basis of Union: How Well Does it Stand up to Scrutiny?" *Uniting Church Studies* 17, no 2 (2011): 55-66; Andrew Dutney, "Flexible and Free: An Ecclesiology of Change," *Uniting Church Studies* 21, no 1 (2017): 9-18; Rebecca Lindsay, "Standing on the cusp with Moses: The Basis of Union, Deuteronomy and Hope," *Uniting Church Studies* 21, no 1 (2017): 19-30.

the participation of people from various parts of the church, the majority of presenters at the first conference were established academic theologians. This shifted somewhat at the second conference with the participation of, among others, the then Chair of the Uniting Aboriginal and Islander Christian Congress, Rev Ken Sumner, and some younger leaders of the Uniting Church.

The 2021 conference retained the academic style, but a little more loosely. And, continuing the shift at the 2014 conference, the majority of the presenters were not established academic theologians. They also reflected an even greater cultural and linguistic diversity than the presenters at the previous conferences, and nearly all were either born after union or had joined the Uniting Church long after 1977. New horizons of engagement with the *Basis* were opened up. The theme, "The *Basis* at 50: Its present and future," directed the presentations away from the history of the document and its formation. Instead, it shifted the attention towards both its reception in the life of the Church and to questions about how the document might still function. Of course, matters of exposition were not bypassed (see below), but the filters through which those expositions were presented were significantly shaped by contemporary issues of race, gender, culture and colonisation. A backwards glance was not ignored, but the ongoing legacy of certain ambiguities in the *Basis* was brought into focus.

Before introducing the chapters that follow, a little more needs to be said about the various voices heard at the 2021 conference. Not all who presented papers at the conference were able to revise their presentations for publication. These included a seminar paper on reading the *Basis* in the context of the climate crisis and one on the legacy of the *Basis* for the understanding of lay ministry (presented by Jessica Morthorpe and Damian Palmer respectively). Those themes were important to the conference and helped to shape the conversations that ensued. This was also the case with a panel conversation on "Receiving the *Basis*: CALD experiences." At this session, Assembly President-elect Rev Charissa Suli hosted a conversation with Rev Bea Skippen, Rev Cyrus Kung and Sione Hehepoto. A second panel, chaired by Assembly President, Sharon Hollis, explored the way the *Basis* shapes and/or limits the UCA's engagement with its contemporary context. The panellists for this conversation were Rev Radhika Sukumar-White, Rev Stu Cameron, Rev Dr Sally Douglas, Rev (Deacon) Sandy Boyce, Dr Janice McRandal, Rev Linda Hanson and Dr Damian Palmer.[4] Once all these presenters are added to those whose work is included in this book, it will be evident that the conference drew together a community which reflected a wide cross section of ages, cultures, theologies and roles in the church.

Whilst not an exhaustive reflection of the conference, the papers contained in this volume provide a good snapshot of the range of issues which were addressed. It also includes three other papers not presented at the conference, but which also add to the 50th anniversary discussion. The resultant selection of papers reflect the variety of styles adopted in the original presentations. Some are more obviously seminar-type academic papers, whereas some are reflective and invitational, and some are more explicitly hortatory. Just as the conference itself was not intended solely for academics, neither is this volume. The papers represent the diversity of the Uniting Church, and this diverse engagement with the *Basis* is indeed a gift to the Church. Overall, there is a narrative in this volume: it moves from the lived experience in the land, to critical engagements and interpretative conversations, and through to the future of the Uniting Church. Therefore, the papers are divided into four sections and a postscript.

The first section consists of two papers under the heading of **Indigenous Engagements**. Maratja Dhamarrandi's "The *Basis of Union*: a Yolŋu Perspective" was the opening address at the conference. Marajta invites us into the Yolŋu concept of *rom* (law)

---

4 Some of these presentations, and others reflecting on the fiftieth anniversary of the *Basis*, are available at "The *Basis* at 50," Uniting Church in Australia Assembly: Growing in Faith" https://uniting.church/the-basis-at-50-reflections -and-responses/

as a way of expanding the idea of the "guidance" which the *Basis* offers. He explains how *rom* leads to *dukkar* (path). The richness and the inter-relationship of these terms, as they are outlined in Maratja's chapter, do not yield to any easy translation into English concepts or conventional Western theological concepts. In fact, it broadens the interpretative framework of the *Basis*. This provides the occasion for Second Peoples to engage this First Nations' insight into what is there in the *Basis* but which is actually obscured by Western conceptual frameworks. The prayer with which Maratja's paper concludes invites us into the openness necessary to gain that insight, discern the path ahead, and go in God's way.

The second paper in this section was jointly written by Ken Sumner and Michelle Cook and is one of the chapters that emerged from outside the conference. In fact, it was presented at the 2014 *Basis* conference in Sydney, but it had never been published. The issues it addresses are no less significant today than they were in 2014 and properly belong to the 50th anniversary conversation. The paper, "What good is it to me if I can't eat it: Grounding the *Basis of Union* in our lived experience," revolves around the authors' conversation as they explore three questions: "Where am I in this story?", "How do we read the *Basis*?", and "How do we ground the *Basis* in our lived experience?" They draw attention to the eclipse of First Peoples in the *Basis*, and also to how the knowledge of this absence in its own way draws attention to the pain of stolen children and the violent suppression of language. Moreover, they also draw out how this absence has impacted, and continues to impact, the interpretation and appropriation of other parts of the *Basis*, notably the meaning of "in Australia," "reconciliation," and the "fellowship of Christ's sufferings." They argue that the *Basis* must be read along with, and through the filter of, the Covenanting Statement and the Revised Preamble to the Constitution in order to correct this absence and its impact on the reading and reception of the *Basis*.

The second section of the collection is headed, **Exposition**. It includes five papers. The section heading may not fully capture the work done in these chapters, but they belong together as the chapters which are focused on close readings of selected texts of the *Basis*. They are not, however, abstract expositions: they variously reflect cultural, ideological, historical and ecclesiological awareness as they engage their respective texts. The first two papers in this section were the two keynote addresses at the conference.

In "The Call to Transcend Racial Boundaries: An Analysis of the Language in Paragraph 2 of the *Basis of Union* ," Joy Han demonstrates the racially-constructed notion of "Asia and Pacific" found in that paragraph and how its reference to "transcending racial boundaries" reinforces the absence of any reference to Australia's First Peoples. Drawing on various postcolonial theorists, she argues that the "white-centric and Eurocentric conceits" embedded in these elements of the *Basis* continue to be reflected in the UCA's contemporary discourses, not least in the discourse of multiculturalism. She argues that at least some of the resources to correct these problems can be found in the *Basis* itself, particularly paragraphs 3 and 4.

Liam Miller, in "Tradition in the *Basis*: Silences, Exclusions and Openings" offers a very close reading of the different postures towards the received tradition that are manifest in different parts of the *Basis*. Framing his argument by Marcella Althaus-Reid's critique of the West's "T-Theology" and its colonising silencing of other theologies, Miller argues that whereas the early paragraphs of the *Basis* reflect an orientation to just such a T-Theology which is simply to be received, the later paragraphs (specifically 9, 10 and 11) loosen this orientation. The key theological shift he identifies, and which points to this loosening, is a shift from an emphasis on the agency of the Christ to that of the church. This shift allows for the negotiation of "particular postures" towards the tradition and the legitimation of human agency in confessing Christ in fresh words and deeds. This opens the door to giving voice to those not only at the margins, but to those who are "off the maps of those who enshrined the Tradition."

Albeit from a very different perspective and for different reasons, Michael Earl, in his "Bound and Free: The legacy of the *Basis of Union* for Ordination," similarly explores the relationship within the *Basis* between tradition and fresh confession. In tackling the issue of ordination, he addresses a topic which, as he points out, has provoked "repetitive and wearying" discussions and continually presents itself as a "critical and conflicted aspect" of the UCA's life. He traces this conflict to an ambiguity in Paragraph 14 and its recognition of variations in the types and duration of ministries and its acknowledgment that union coincided with a "period of reconsideration of traditional forms of the ministry." Could this be extended to licence the abandonment of ordination? This ambiguity, he argues, is not just related to ordination itself, but it also feeds confusion about the nature of lay ministry. Yet, Earl maintains paragraph 14 is straining to say something which honours the legacy of the Reformed/Evangelical understanding of ordination which fed into the Uniting Church. So understood, the threefold task classically linked to ordination – preaching, presiding and pastoring – is "laden with creative promise for an expansive, engaged and empowered witness."

John Evans' paper, "The *Basis of Union* and the 'Uniting' in the Uniting Church in Australia," was not presented at the conference, but emerged, in part, from Evans' involvement in the Uniting Church/Lutheran dialogue and his own participation in the conference. Confronting the fact that the vision of further unions intimated in the *Basis* has never been realised, Evans identifies other understandings of unity which are found, or at least implied, in the *Basis*. He acknowledges the various contextual changes that have worked against further unions, but argues that the impulse for unity amongst Christians, so central to the *Basis*, should not be lost even if its retrieval will take forms other than organic union. He takes several key phrases from various paragraphs of the *Basis* to explore how such unity might show itself in, for instance, shared theological work, shared missional engagement, and reflections on church law. And making up for an absence in the *Basis*, he proposes a retrieval of the idea of concordats, such as that which the Joint Commission on Church Union proposed that the Uniting Church should have with the Church of South India, but which was not included in the 1971 *Basis*.

The Christological focus of the *Basis* has long been recognised, and it is often taken to have rendered the document pneumatologically deficient. In her paper, "On Not Losing the Way: the Holy Spirit in the *Basis of Union*," Ennis Macleod addresses this accusation head on. The paper is based on a textual analysis through which she presents a full list of references to the Holy Spirit in the *Basis*. Macleod unearths what is at least an implicit pneumatology which revolves around gifts, power and unity. But she also identifies some striking omissions and anomalies. These include the Spirit's absence from paragraph 11 with its summons to the confession of faith in fresh words and deeds. She also notes the absence of any reference to the Spirit in creation and that the nexus of Spirit–giftedness–service leaves the question of personal sanctification unaddressed in the *Basis*. Nevertheless, she maintains that the *Basis*'s confession of the promise of the Spirit to the church is its own invitation for the Uniting Church to engage the broader work of the Spirit. She points to the adoption of the Revised Preamble as a step in that direction.

We turn now to the four papers of the third section of paper, **Cross-Cultural Engagements**. In one sense, these engagements with the *Basis* are more narrative in style and draw from the experience of particular members of CALD communities within the Uniting Church. They reveal how the *Basis* provides hope, poses limitations, and presents opportunities as the Uniting Church seeks to make good on its declaration to be a multicultural church.

Ji Zhang, in "Translating the *Basis of Union*: Learning from Heart Languages," gives an overview of the Assembly project, "The *Basis of Union* in Heart Languages." The *Basis* has so far been translated into 10 of the 45 languages which are used across the congregations of the Uniting Church. The gift of this project is not just that of making the document available to the UCA's various linguistic communities, it is also in the wrestling and understanding offered to the whole church that comes through the process of translation, interpretation and intercultural exchange as the meaning of key claims and words are expanded and challenged in the encounter between different linguistic and conceptual worlds. As the translations collectively show, this plurality of languages and worldviews cannot be reduced to a unity of sameness, nor a mere togetherness. Paying particular attention to the Chinese, Fijian and Tongan translations, Zhang points out that the work of translation has become a "journey of discovery," not least into the reality of the relationship of unity and mission which is a central theme of the *Basis*. Then, Zhang reflects on "the gift of the Spirit" in the *Basis* and the spirit of creation in the *Preamble* and invites the audience to read these documents together in celebration of the Triune God's unity in diversity.

Hee Won Chang's "Cultural Identity and the *Basis of Union*: a non-white migrant musing" begins by addressing issues of cultural identity. She refers to her own resistance to being pigeonholed and of the need, as she says, "to find a language about myself." By analogy, the Uniting Church is often pigeonholed and similarly faces a challenge to find a language about itself. This, she argues, is even more acute in the Pandemic and post-Pandemic context, i.e. in a "world turned upside down." She turns to the *Basis* as a way for the Church finding its story in this context. With particular reference to the *Basis*'s language of "pilgrim people," she draws on parallels to the migrant experience to warn against any romanticising of this image: "If you ask any migrant, they will tell you the pains of journeying in the new land are often loaded with frustration, anger, deep sadness and confusion." Framing this further by the *Basis*'s locating the church in this time between Christ's resurrection and the final consummation, she envisages the church "perched on the margins."

Whilst not closely engaged with the text of the *Basis*, Jason Kioa, in "The Role of the Tongan National Conference in relation to the *Basis of Union*," tells something of the history of this Conference and the challenges it has faced. He acknowledges that it "took some years for the Tongans to appreciate the richness of the *Basis of Union*." Kioa wonders what might have been if the *Basis* (and the preceding ecclesial journey it represents) had been multicultural from the outset. Yet, he also says that the Tongan National Conference "has found its life and existence in the *Basis*." Against this, however, Kioa argues the Tongan National Conference and the other National Conferences occupy an uncertain space in the Uniting Church. Nevertheless, he uses the well-known practice, the unfolding mat for *talanoa*, to symbolise an open and unfolding unity. The Tongan National Conference can become the mat that often rolls out so that the Tongan diaspora and intercultural community of the Uniting Church can sit down for a great *talanoa*. This offers a deeper and contextual conversation about our life together as the Second Peoples in the land of the First Peoples of Australia. His paper raises important questions for the polity of a multicultural church and it is an open question as to what extent the *Basis* impedes or advances this.

The fourth section of papers, **Conference Reflections**, is quite brief and consists of revised versions of three reflections given at the end of the conference as three invited "listeners" engaged a selection of the issues they had identified during the day.

In "Being Guided by the Basis of Union" Andrew Johnson explores some of the background that produced the language of "guidance" and asks what this concept means in practice. He warns against, among other things, weaponising the *Basis* by using it as a proof text. Constructively, he argues that it has more flexibility than some of its critics allege. At the same time, in acknowledging its incompleteness, he suggests it must be read in tandem with various post-union documents. In being guided by it we should treat it as a set of navigational aids.

Sean Winter, an English Baptist minister who has served in the Uniting Church in theological education for over a decade, reflected on what he heard at the conference in "The Basis of Union Through Baptist Eyes." The conference highlighted for him the way that the *Basis* provides a tool for "ordering the vision and life of the church around those things that are central to the gospel." As such it becomes a resource for keeping alert to what keeps the church faithful, just as it helps the church see when it has become unfaithful. For the same reasons, it draws us into "relationships of difference" and provokes "change and renewal."

Assembly President, Sharon Hollis, built her reflection around the suggestion, raised at the conference, that the church now needed something like a "Basis for Journeying," perhaps as a replacement of the *Basis of Union*. In considering this, she noted the way various presenters had revealed, even in their critical readings of it, that the *Basis* "offers theological wisdom that is both grounded in and open to the questions and challenges of the current time." A document that does this should not be easily set aside. But if the time comes when a new document might sit beside the *Basis*, we should be careful about whose voices it reflects. Among other things, she writes, "Let any such document be multi-lingual, filled with the knowledge and wisdom of First Nations people, and the Second Peoples who speak many languages an inhabit multiple cultures."

The *Postscript* to this volume is the third of the papers to have emerged from outside the conference, and it too addresses the future of the *Basis*. It is a revised version of a public lecture, "A Basis for Continuing," first presented by Peter Hobson on November 18th 2021. It was part of *The Cooperative*'s Albert Street Lectures at the Albert Street Uniting Church, Brisbane, in its own acknowledgment of the 50th anniversary. Hobson sets out to "honour the enduring legacy of the *Basis of Union* and its defining qualities by daring to look to the next 50 years to begin imagining the role of the *Basis of Union* in influencing the generations to come." In this act of imagining, Hobson finds impulses within the

*Basis* to address such matters as postcolonial theologies and ethics, gender and sexual inclusivity, care for the environment, theological diversity, the practice of public theology, and kingdom – rather than empire-building.

As will be evident from these overviews, the chapters that follow provide rich fare for their readers. As the editors, we are delighted to see these insights now reach a wider audience. Together, we believe that they constitute a new chapter in the reception and interpretation of the *Basis*. Whilst the issues addressed do not reflect all the conversations occurring in the UCA, the authors have posed a wide range of new questions, offered new interpretations and established a more varied horizon for the reception and use of this seminal document. None of the authors has read it uncritically. And nearly all of them have read and interpreted it alongside other significant documents produced post-union, especially "The Covenant Statement," "We are a Multicultural Church" and the "Revised Preamble to the Constitution." Others have read it in context of some of the more highly-charged contemporary critical theories. Others have read it in conversation with the Uniting Church's own theological heritage.

For half a century, the *Basis* has been an anchoring document for nurturing and sustaining a theological culture across the life of the Church. Certainly, this book demonstrates that the *Basis* has been a fertile document, involving us in an ongoing conversation. The contributors to this volume warrant our thanks for opening a new chapter in this conversation.

# Indigenous Engagements

# 1

# The *Basis of Union* as *Rom*: A Yolŋu Perspective[1]

## Maratja Dhamarrandji

My name is Maratja Dhamarrandji. I am a Yolŋu man and a Christian man. I'm body, soul and spirit. I'm connected to the past, the now and the future. The holistic ministry very much fits in my DNA. First, to accept the fact that I am a Yolŋu man and that I have a Yolŋu world view give glory to God Bapa, God-Waŋarr, the maker of all things. I would like to acknowledge my mentors Rev Dr Waŋkul (Djiniyini) Gondarra, Rev Rronaŋ Garrawurra and Bapa Jo Mowandjil, George Danyŋumba Dhurrkay, Timothy Buthimaŋ Dhurrkay, Bill Bapawun Dhamarrandji (Father), Jean Gumdjirryirr Dhurrkay, Dorothy Wanymuli Dhamarrandji (Mukul Bapa – Aunty). I also acknowledge Howard and Felicity Amery and Nungalinya College, who helped shape me into the ministry of Deacon in the Uniting Church. Lastly, I would like to thank Dorothy Gapany Gumbula (my wife) and my three children, Samantha Rapark, Theresa Mathayalma and Justin Warrŋulwuy and all my grandchildren and great-grandchildren.

One of the means through which the ancestors shape who Yolŋu are, is the *Gurruṯu* (relationship) culture or system with the *Mälk* culture (also known as 'skin culture'). The Yolŋu universe is divided into two halves (or moieties) – Dhuwa and Yirritja – and *Gurruṯu-Mälk* culture prescribes how the two halves may interweave. The *Gurruṯu-Mälk* culture applies to all members of creation: humans, land and sea creatures, plants, and all other living

---

1 Some of the material in this chapter is taken from Maratja Dharmarrandji with Jione Havea, "*Mäna / Buḻ'manydji* calls for Wounded theologies," in *Bordered Bodies, Bothered Voices: Native and Migrant Theologies*, ed. Jione Havea (Eugene: Pickwick, 2022)

creatures. Each member of creation is a half of a different member, with the pairing determined by the *Gurruṯu-Mälk* culture. Each creature in the Yolŋu universe has the privilege to receive a partner, which the *Gurruṯu-Mälk* culture determines to come from *the other half*. *Gurruṯu-Mälk* explains whom one might marry, the obligations that one has to one's family and community, and gives direction in how and with whom we might develop kinship.

When we think of our life as the Church, it is important to know this overall *rom (law)*, the *Basis of Union*, and the *dhukarr*, the path, of this *rom*. It is critical, as members of the Uniting Church, that we understand the whole *rom*. We need to know what the *Basis of Union* means for us. We need to know what the checks and balances are, the accountability and transparency, of the *rom*. We need to know the requirements of this *rom*. What does it mean? What are the checks and balances and the requirements of the law?

The *rom* is in our *Yolŋu* culture. We have to at least have some basic understanding of the *rom*, in order to survive and relate to each other. In the *Yolŋu rom*, we have the basis for right relationship ever since we are *yothu* (small, baby). We know our requirements about what not to do and what to do. We were taught that and given examples about that early in our life. We acknowledge *rom* through the bush university, but in hindsight what they were saying, *yolŋu-mala*, was we are to respect the law, the *rom*. When Jesus said about that golden rule – do unto others what you would have them do unto you – the Yolŋu perspective is basically that in its entirety. We follow the *rom* so we can be accountable and try to find the *dhukarr*, the pathway. All the ceremonies and bush universities are shown to us and taught to us by the elders so that we know the *rom* and follow the *dhukarr*. The *gurruṯu* system, *Yothu-yindi*, *märi-gutharra*, all these checks and balances are so we can follow that *dhukarr* and have the fulfilment of the *rom*.

It is like this with Church law. God's provision, his providence, in the *Basis of Union*, reminds us to respect and honour and go through the *dhukarr* – the *manymak dhukarr* (good or right path). That is why God gave us the Scriptures, so that we can find the right way. There are a lot of stories in the Bible about ups and downs and failures, but God, in his sovereignty and power, made a way for us. We are here, God has made a way for us and we have to be accountable and make sure that we are honouring God and being obedient. That is part of the responsibility that we have.

It is very important for *Yolŋu* people to know this *Basis of Union*. Sometimes there are a lot of words here, difficult English words, that make it hard. It is important for *Yolŋu* to have a basic understanding about the Church, about how we are accountable to God, each other and other Churches.

We are family. We are God's family. It is good to have this path to follow. By respecting and honouring we are pleasing God. It is an imperative, a command and we have to work out what to do and what not to do with our mind and heart and actions. Our actions speak louder than words. So how can we study this whole story and practice that in our life. Not just individually, but corporately, as a family, practice *raypirri* – discipline for the soul and spirit – individually and *bukmak* (all together). Everyone who is called at once to the Church, to the ekklesia, we are also called to be going on that path, that *dhukarr*, to God's way. We know that *Waŋarr* (God) before that mission came. We know about God's way, and we have to adjust and work out what is *manymak* and what is *yaka manymak* for us, our society, and the missionaries. We have to find that balance.

There is some requirement in the law for all of us, whether it is Yolŋu law, balanda law, or God's law. We are accountable. And all the nuts and bolts are in this *Basis of Union*. We need to unpack it and talk about it and share it with our people, so we can understand in a Yolŋu way.

The *gurruṯu* system tells us about our responsibility in the family. It is undergirded by respect and honour, making sure we go through the right way in the eyes of *Yolŋu rom*. It is a bit like that too when we study the whole bible, the *rom* of *Garray* (Lord Jesus). It is very important for us to unpack, comprehend, and see the *bukmak dhawu* (whole story). Then we can be in a better place when we are doing some preaching, teaching and even pastoral care. As leaders of the church, we have to know how to be accountable to God and the Church. We need to work together for the Church to go on the *dhukarr* that God provided for us through his son Jesus Christ. His Holy Spirit working in us teaches us the way of God. We have to get our story so that it lines up with the *Basis of Union*. Let us hold hands collaboratively so that we can have that basis, that understanding, for our life together.

Prayer:

*God-Waŋarr Bäpa bokmanayŋu djiwarrŋur*
*Ga ŋanapurru ga Balanda ga bukmak*
*nhuŋu creation marrkapmirr, seen and unseen*
*Bukmak nhakun Garray marrkapmirr*
We are your creation
*Garray marrkapmirr* (Lord beloved one)

Thank you, Lord, for this time we've been able to understand and study the *Basis of Union*
That we can be more knowledgeable and become more responsible for how we do Church.
May the elders and leaders be able to know our way,
The pathway that developed through the church and the leaders
Remembering the centrality of Christ
and God's provision, God's providence for *bukmakku* (all of us).

Help us to be enthused and excited *nhuŋu rom ga raypirri' ga* discipline
(for your law and discipline).
*Garray marrkapmirr* teach us all about honour and respect
for *nhuŋu* (you) and for the whole Church.
Help the Church universal, *bukmak* (all) Church
*nhaltjan napurr dhu* respecting *nhuna* (you) so we can follow your ways.

We so *yaka manymak*, we fall short, for we all have sinned.
We have missed the mark *Garray marrkapmirr*

28

Thank you for all *nhuŋu* provision *Garray marrkapmirr,*
*nhuŋu* providence *Garray marrkapmirr*
You've given us through your Word and for Creeds and for the
Uniting Church.
Thank you Lord for forming this church so that we can follow the
rom of the Uniting Church
so that we can go in your way, *Garray marrkapmirr*

Help each and every one of us *bukmaknha*
*napurr dhu maryŋithirr,* respect *ga* honour you
And respecting one another as *nhyuŋu* family, *Godku* family,
*Garray marrkapmirr*
Open *napurruŋ* (our) hearts, eyes *ga* minds to see *nhuŋu* activity,
*nhuŋu* love at work in the life of *nhuŋu* people in the Church
In Jesus' name, *napurr* (we) pray, Amen.

## 2

# What Good Is It to Me If I Can't Eat It? Grounding the *Basis of Union* in Our Lived experience

Ken Sumner and Michelle Cook

## Introduction

The *Basis of Union*, to quote Davis McCaughey, "points the Churches to the places where faith can be found, where faith can be renewed and where faith can constantly be nourished."[1] This is a bold claim for a document conceived and created at the edges of the British Empire, as Australia mainly was thought of in the Menzies era. The framers of the document very clearly understood it as "*the* statement of Faith and Order which would guide the ongoing life of the Uniting Church."[2] In various Assembly discussions and statements, the *Basis of Union* has been invoked to ensure that the Uniting Church is 'on the way to the promised end' (Para 18) and has not "[lost] the way."[3] The *Basis* has become the standard by which all theological, ecclesiological and ministerial work in the

---

1 J. Davis McCaughey, *The Basis of Union: A Commentary*, ed. Andrew Dutney (Sydney, Australia: Assembly of the Uniting Church in Australia, 2016), 18.

2 *The Status, Authority and Role of the Basis of Union within the Uniting Church in Australia: a discussion paper issued by the Assembly* Sydney, NSW: Uniting Church in Australia National Assembly, 1996. Our emphasis.

3 The full quote from paragraph 3 of the *Basis*: "On the way Christ feeds the Church with Word and Sacraments, and it has the gift of the Spirit in order that it may not lose the way." Examples from the Assembly are the themes 'Forward Together' 8th Assembly 1997. In 1997 the UCA Constitution was also amended through the addition of a new clause (Assembly Minute 97.37.02) to specify the role of the *Basis* as one of guidance. In addition, liturgies of the church were required to have references to the *Basis of Union*, particularly in ordination rites (Assembly Minute 97.37.03). The Presbytery of Nepean also wrote to the Assembly regarding church structures and inconsistencies with the *Basis of Union*. (Appendix B). In 2000, the 9th Assembly a "Statement

Uniting Church is measured. While the *Basis* is a document to treasure and be guided by, it does not tell the whole story of the Uniting Church in Australia. There are aspects of our history in this land that are obscured by this document.

In this paper we will ask a series of questions in order to highlight what has been obscured. We will be asking: Where am I in this story?, How do we read the *Basis*? and How do we ground the *Basis* in our lived experience? First, we ask, where am I in this story? We will offer our respective answers to this question.

## Where am I in this story?

What do you picture when you hear or read this first sentence of the *Basis of Union*?

> The Congregational Union of Australia, the Methodist Church of Australasia and the Presbyterian Church of Australia, in fellowship with the whole Church Catholic, and seeking to bear witness to that unity which is both Christ's gift and will for the Church, hereby enter into union under the name of the Uniting Church in Australia.

*Ken Sumner:*

When I hear or read this first sentence of the *Basis*, there is a flood of memories. I hear the churches and their impact on First Peoples in the missions. I feel the pain of First Peoples, the stolen children, and the violent suppression of language. I think of the dormitory system where children were told not to speak Ngarrindjeri, only

---

of Unity and Diversity" was affirmed which references the understanding of Scripture in the *Basis* (Assembly Minute 00.25.03). These are only a selection of the minutes in which the *Basis of Union* has been used as the standard for practice, for ministry, for theology or for ecclesiology. Michelle's experience of each Assembly since 2009 suggest that the *Basis of Union*, is sometimes used as a conditional phrase to amend proposals and ensure adherence to the tradition.

English. I think of our lands, now mostly covered with farms and holiday homes for the wealthy around Victor Harbour and Goolwa and Meningie. Raukkan, my home, is in the middle of our lands.

I look for my DNA here in this document. I am searching for our songlines. I want to be affirmed as a valued and important part of the church, but I cannot see our tracks. You might say, 'It says we, it says all,' but what I hear is 'them and us'. We First Peoples have historically not been included in such conversations. The 'we' and 'all' you read as including everyone, for us has been a lived experience of exclusion. The stories of the Ngarrindjeri experience with British law and land regulations showed us that we, although understood to be under the law, did not have the benefits and protections of that law.[4]

When I first read the *Basis*, during my college training, it did not have this same impact. This time around, it is different. I see what is here, and I also notice what is missing. I can hear the voices calling and reminding me of our stories, and I cannot separate the history of my peoples from this reading of the *Basis*. I keep on asking, 'Where is my story?'

*Michelle Cook:*

When Ken shared these thoughts with me, I realised that I had never reflected on the first sentence of the *Basis*. To me, this first sentence was an historical statement that had very little relevance to someone born in 1975. For instance, I only had to think about the Presbyterian, Congregationalist or Methodist Church when I had to prepare worship at my home church. One of our worshipping communities was known for its love of Wesleyan hymns. This congregation did not appreciate me suggesting singing from the Psalter. That was something for the Presbyterians. Reading earlier documents from the Joint Commission on Church Union I was struck by this statement:

---

4 Graham Jenkin, *Conquest of the Ngarrindjerri*, 2nd ed. (Port Macleay: Raukkan Publishers, 1995), especially chapter 3.

He who would recall us simply to be better Congregationalists, Methodists, or Presbyterians would call us out of the twentieth century; and as for us, we will not go. The way forward must be with the living Christ, the Lord of this perplexing world.[5]

It takes great courage to relinquish the certainties of a particular tradition to move into new territory. It was the courage of those who fought for union that inspired me. The story of my own local church, which united the Presbyterians and Methodists in 1975, was a testament to this journey and is reflected in the first sentence of the *Basis*.

## How do we Read the *Basis*?

*Reflecting deeper and wider*

Reading through the *Basis* together has opened a wider story that is not adequately referenced or witnessed to in the *Basis*. In paragraph 2, we read:

> [The Uniting Church in Australia] believes that Christians in Australia are called to bear witness to a unity of faith and life in Christ which transcends cultural and economic, national and racial boundaries, and to this end the Uniting Church commits itself to seek special relationships with Churches in Asia and the Pacific.

In the *Basis*, we specifically acknowledge the geographic location of Australia in Asia and the Pacific. Yet, we fail to recognise the invasion and colonisation of that location and the consequent dispossession of the First Peoples of this land. The framers of the *Basis* were insistent on forming a church that could witness in and to this new location, however, they did not recognise the first residents of the lands. In fact, the only mention of First Peoples by

---

5 FOTC, 15.

the Joint Commission on Church Union is in 'The Faith of the Church':

> Once more, in putting their own houses in order by renewing their grasp on the Faith in its wholeness, the Churches of Australia will equip themselves for their part in preaching the gospel to the ends of the earth and to the end of time. Whether in her own industrial or rural society in Australia, or in the fulfilment of obligations undertaken towards the aboriginals within her borders, or in the edification of the Church overseas, the Church in Australia needs a fuller and clearer grasp of the gospel, and all that that implies.[6]

First Peoples here are not part of the church, but rather, objects of the church's obligations. There is no further exploration of what these obligations are and why they exist.

Davis McCaughey's 1980 commentary gives a brief insight into the vision of the *Basis* for this new church in Australia:

> Within our own border, in Australia itself, there are opportunities for bearing witness to a fellowship in Christ which 'transcends cultural and economic, national and racial boundaries': aboriginals [sic], white settlers predominantly from the British Isles, ethnic groups from Europe, the Middle East, Asia and the Pacific must now learn to sit down together in an anticipation of life in the kingdom of God.[7]

Here McCaughey is explicit that the transcending of boundaries includes intercultural boundaries, however, the impacts of colonisation on the First Peoples of the lands are not acknowledged. Instead, First Peoples are noted within a group of ethnicities, implying the priority of overcoming 'racial' boundaries, rather than addressing

---

6  FOTC, 39.
7  J. Davis McCaughey, *Commentary on the Basis of Union*. (Melbourne: JBCE, 1980), para 2.

injustice. Confronting the history of colonisation is not mentioned in this commentary.[8]

Such an omission in the foundational document of the Uniting Church demands that we grapple with the question of the identity of a church that names itself as being 'in Australia'. Since union, there has been much conversation about how we imagine ourselves as such a church. Significant for our reading of the *Basis* now is an understanding of the fundamental shift in academic and public discourse that has occurred since the *Basis* was being written and voted on. These changes are characterised by movement from the universal to the particular, from the global to the local and from sameness to difference. A brief outline of this change is given below.

In the 19th Century, the study of religion had become dominated by the assumptions and methods of the Enlightenment. Scholars of the Enlightenment stressed universality and objective knowledge in the search for truth. The researcher or theologian, to achieve objectivity, was to be silent in both the conduct of research and the reporting of results. By the second half of the twentieth century, however, hermeneutics as a discipline had made a distinct turn to the subject. The critical hermeneutic task for the researcher, heavily influenced by the work of Hans-Georg Gadamer, became the elucidation of the intersection of the horizons of text/s and interpreter/s.[9] By the 1970s, with the emphasis on the subject/interpreter dominating philosophy, there was a concomitant increased awareness of world-views other than

---

8 It could be argued that the language of "colonisation" was not commonplace in the 1970s and 1980s. However, the 1960s witnessed the gaining of independence of former colonies of Europe in Africa and Asia. In the 1960s and 1970s, Australia itself saw the rise of the Land Rights Movement in which the UCA and its predecessors were intimately involved. The new Preamble of the Uniting Church constitution explicitly addresses the omission of this narrative from the "law" documents of the Uniting Church.

9 See Richard R Osmer, *Practical Theology: An Introduction* (Grand Rapids, Michigan: William B Eerdmans Publishing Company, 2009), 23.

those dominant in Western theology.[10] This was catalysed in the West by the rise of African and Asian national independence and the burgeoning of Christian churches in the majority world.

The *Basis of Union* itself has claims to be a universal document, a statement of faith that seeks to 'transcend' difference and restate the core faith of the church. However, it was finished just at the time when local, contextual theologies were starting to dominate theological conversations.[11] This claim to universality has implications for how we use the document in conversation, argument, change, and renewal. For example, should the *Basis* be the standard by which all other theological documents *must* be assessed? Or can it be used to inspire conversation and action into 'fresh words and deeds'? Is it to be used as a conversation partner or an ahistorical benchmark? Below we explore two identities claimed by the *Basis* that are important in navigating our reading of the document.

## How do we read the *Basis of Union*?

*Identity as 'church in Australia'*

In *Exclusion and Embrace*, Miroslav Volf builds on the work of Jacques Derrida on European identity, writing, "Europe's past is full of the worst of violence committed in the name of European identity".[12] Replacing 'Europe' with Australia, confronts us with

---

10  See Klauspeter Blaser, "Multicultural Christianity: A Project for Liberation. The Meaning of the Conflict North-south for Theology and Our Churches", *International Review of Mission* 72, no. 326 (1993): 203-216 and Harold A Netland, "Introduction: Globalization and Theology Today," in *Globalizing Theology: Belief and Practice in An Era of World Christianity*, ed. Craig Ott and Harold A Netland (Grand Rapids, Michigan: Baker Academic, 2006), 24.

11  See David Bosch, *Transforming Mission: Paradigm Shifts in the Theology of Mission 20th Anniversary Edition* (Maryknoll, New York: Orbis, 2012).

12  Miroslav Volf, *Exclusion and Embrace: A Theological Exploration of Identity, Otherness and Reconciliation* (Nashville: Abingdon Press, 1996), 17.

the violent reality of our own history. The colonisation of Australia was bound up in the need to establish and maintain the British Empire. Concerns about other European powers inhabiting the "great south land" as well as the need for a penal colony after the loss of the United States were paramount in the decision to utilise the information from the Cook voyages of 1770.

The original instructions to the colony emphasised showing "kindness to the Natives" yet there was no recognition that this land belonged to them.[13] This kindness did not last beyond Governor Phillip's tenure as Governor. Indeed the presence of "Natives" were eventually seen as a hindrance to the expansion of the colony. Eventually the lands of Australia were recognised as "waste lands" and terra nullius. That is, not productive, and therefore, not inhabited and consequently, available for lease or purchase by colonists from the crown. The First Peoples were viewed as less than human and there was indiscriminate killing of clans and poisoning of food stuffs and provisions that went unpunished. The British Government and, subsequently, the Australian Government are responsible for inherently racist and discriminatory practises towards the First Peoples of these lands. To be a church "in Australia" means wrestling with this history and our place in it.

*Identity as church in Australia – belonging to Christ*

One of the most striking features of the *Basis of Union* is its Christological emphasis. The Church only exists and survives because of the risen crucified Christ (BOU, 3)). Christ is the one who "reaches out to command people's attention and awaken faith" (BOU, 4). It is in Jesus Christ, through the power of the Holy Spirit, not the Church, that we find our meaning. Thus, Christ is the great unifier of the diverse peoples who make up his community, the Church. However, as Clive Pearson notes:

---

13 *Governor Phillip's Instructions 25 April 1787* accessed July 9, 2022, https://www.foundingdocs.gov.au/resources/transcripts/nsw2_doc_1787.pdf

Are we being held together too simply by the theological gloss of us all being 'in Christ'? Are our cultural specificities, in effect, being denied or subsumed under a Pauline-like formula: In Christ, there is neither Vietnamese-Australian nor Fijian-Australian; there is neither Aboriginal nor sixth-generation Anglo-Celt/Anglo-Australian ... in Christ we are all one?[14]

Highlighting our oneness in Christ can lead to us glossing or smoothing over the differences in our lived experiences, especially when confronting issues of justice. The default understanding of oneness in Christ can be that assumed by the dominant culture. In contrast, Anthony Reddie, in *Is God Colour-Blind?* states:

> The body of Christ is about recognising difference. The body should be concerned with providing opportunities for all marginalised and oppressed peoples to have their choices, preferences and identities recognised, and for the existing power structures to be overturned in order that those elements can be realised.[15]

In Australia, the dominant narrative has been a peaceful transition into nationhood and a "fair-go" available for all. To hear the stories of First Peoples, reminds us that, though in Christ, there is no Jew or Greek, there is an imperative to grapple with the injustice inherent in our very existence. To be part of the Body of Christ, as Reddie suggests, means that we are called to "step outside ourselves," into an "others" world and to "make space for the changing other in ourselves."[16] It is through Christ that we are able to experience the "pledge and foretaste of that coming reconciliation and renewal which is the end in view for the whole creation" (BOU, 3).

---

14  Clive Pearson, "Criss-Crossing Cultures" in *Faith in a Hyphen: Cross-cultural Theologies Down Under*, ed. Clive Pearson (Adelaide: Open Book Publishing, 2004), 19.

15  Anthony G Reddie, *Is God Colour-Blind? Insights from Black Theology for Christian Ministry* (London: SPCK, 2009), 12.

16  Volf, *Exclusion and Embrace*, 251, 154.

## Grounding the *Basis* in our Lived Experience

*Reading with the Covenant and the Preamble*

What would it mean, then, to read the *Basis of Union*, taking into account what it means to be "in Australia" and reconciled "in Christ"? The Uniting Church in Australia has made significant statements regarding the relationship between First and Second Peoples and the concomitant pursuit of justice and desire for reconciliation. However, it is not usual for the *Basis of Union* to be used as a plumbline in these documents, despite our propensity to add "guided by the *Basis of Union*" into many official church decisions. For example, when discussing changes to doctrine at the Assembly the *Basis of Union* and its expressed desire for Christian unity is invoked to either push for the doctrinal change or to stymie the change.[17] When we bring the Preamble and the Covenant into mutual conversation with the *Basis of Union*, what does God reveal to us about our calling to be a Church in Australia?

*The Fellowship of his sufferings*

> Your ancestors came to us in different ways and we saw little of our caring God in them. They did not come to us as God's will would dictate, but to dispossess us, take our children, rape our women, kill our men and boys and destroy our culture, reject our values and beliefs and ultimately claim our lands as their own.
>
> As a direct result of this violent dispossession, Aboriginal and Torres Strait Islander people have lived as strangers and outcasts in their own land.[18]
>
> The uniting churches were largely silent as the dominant culture of Australia constructed and propagated a distorted

---

17  For examples, see discussions on changes to the Uniting Church understanding of marriage (2012, 2015, 2018), the Uniting Church understanding of the Diaconate (1991, 1994) and the dropping of the Filioque clause from the Nicene Creed in UCA Liturgy (1985).

18  TCS.

version of history that denied this land was occupied, utilised, cultivated and harvested by these First Peopleswho also had complex systems of trade and inter-relationships. As a result of this denial, relationships were broken and the very integrity of the Gospel proclaimed by the churches was diminished.[19]

*Ken Sumner reflects:*

During my tour around the Uniting Church to introduce and advocate for the Preamble, I heard people say, and I still hear people say, "move on". It is important to remind you all that no-one wants to stay in pain and suffering. We are in pain because these events and attitudes that have happened in the past are still happening. It is perplexing to hear people say "move on" in this context. Is this call to move on about "guilt" and wanting to cover over your own complicity in, or apathy towards, the injustices faced by First Peoples? It feels like the call to "forgive and forget" is motivated more by a desire for Second Peoples of many lands to be at peace, rather than address the injustice that disturbs that peace. The purpose of the Covenant and the Preamble, however, is to recognise this history as part of UCA identity.

Reading in the *Basis* that we are called "into the fellowship of his sufferings" reminds all of us, First Peoples and Second Peoples from many lands, that we are part of the one body. When one part of the body is suffering, we are all suffering. And if we are all suffering, we are all committed, and motivated, to relieve that suffering. We are called to show that the "fellowship of his sufferings" are not just words that we quote from the *Basis of Union*. Instead, we are called to show that we feel the sufferings of the world, including the sufferings of First Peoples, and work as an "instrument of Christ" to bear witness to the hope of reconciliation and renewal.

---

19 RevPreamble, paragraph 6.

## The Coming Reconciliation

> We pray that God will guide you together with us in developing a covenant to walk together practically so that the words of your statement may become a tangible expression of His justice and love for all creation.[20]

> [The Uniting Church] entered into an ever deepening covenantal relationship with the Uniting Aboriginal and Islander Christian Congress. This was so that all may see a destiny together, praying and working together for a fuller expression of our reconciliation in Jesus Christ.

> AND THUS the Church celebrates this Covenantal relationship as a foretaste of that coming reconciliation and renewal which is the end in view for the whole creation.[21]

## Michelle Cook reflects:

Both the Covenant Statement and the Preamble to the Constitution implore the Uniting Church to "walk together" with First Peoples, and particularly with the Uniting Aboriginal and Islander Christian Congress. This "walking together" is to be a witness to Christ's work of reconciliation. The aspiration to reconcile affirmed in these statements is hollow without decisions that restore land, share resources and advocate as partners. The notion of "covenant" calls us to a deeper understanding of reconciliation, a reconciliation that can only be manifest when injustice within and without the church is challenged, and we share the abundance of the commonwealth of the church. Such challenge requires the Uniting Church to be willing to "re-negotiate [its] own identity in interaction with the fluid identity of the 'other.'"[22]

We must relinquish power and control in order to re-create the relationship between Congress and the UCA so that we, the church, are a truer reflection of Christ's call to be a 'fellowship of reconciliation' (BOU, 3). It is then that we truly bear witness to the

---

20  TCS
21  RevPreamble, paragraph 10.
22  Volf, *Exclusion and Embrace*, 154.

"coming reconciliation and renewal that is the end in view for the whole creation" (BOU, 3). It is disheartening to witness the effort we put into crafting statements supporting the Covenant and affirming the Sovereignty of First Peoples when these statements are not accompanied by material decisions by the councils of the church. As Rev Bill Hollingsworth said in his response to the Covenant statement read by Jill Tabart in 1994:

> Therefore it would be wrong to just say "I forgive", without reaching a commitment to work together to lay a new foundation upon which we may build a more just future together by ensuring that the Uniting Church plays an active role in providing adequate resources to address the present disadvantages caused by the past injustices and dispossession by the invasion of this country. Your commitment to be practical in seeking to be united in this relationship will be assessed by your decisions to resource the Congress ministry and to be actively involved in ministry alongside and with Aboriginal and Islander people to change the present disadvantage.[23]

In 2018, the Assembly affirmed the sovereignty of First Peoples:

> In the light of:
> (a) the Preamble to the Constitution of Uniting Church in Australia (UCA) which defines sovereignty to be the way in which First Peoples understand themselves to be the traditional owners and custodians, and
> (b) the Statement from the Heart's acknowledgment that sovereignty is a spiritual notion, reflecting the ancestral tie between the land and First Peoples, affirms that the First Peoples of Australia, the Aboriginal and Islander Peoples, are sovereign peoples in this land. [Resolution 65]

A task group was formed to investigate the practical outcomes of such a resolution. This is ongoing work carried by the Walking

---

23 TCF.

together as First and Second Peoples Circle of the Assembly. There has been some movement in elevating the voices of First Peoples in Uniting Church public statements in the services sector through the establishment of the First Peoples' Network in UnitingCare. This has enabled Congress and First Peoples' within UnitingCare to work together in advocacy both to the Uniting Church and to government. The 2022 reconvened Assembly included a renewal of the Covenant and the prominence of First Peoples' in delivering bible reflections. With such networking opportunities and paying heed to Congress voices small steps are being taken to fully live out the call to reconciliation. However, conversations around funding and material resource sharing are still fraught. It is this deeper relationship, of a common-wealth of reconciliation, that we are still to enter.

## Conclusion

The *Basis of Union* is a document that is rightly valued by the Uniting Church. By itself, however, it does not help us address what it means to be a church "in Australia" that "belongs to Christ." The injustice of the dispossession and cultural genocide of First Peoples has no explicit space in this document, even though the churches of the Asia and Pacific are named as important partners for the future. How then can we read the *Basis*? How does it nourish us in our navigation of "following Jesus in invaded space."[24] We must read the *Basis* in concert with the First Peoples of this land. To lift up the rocks to find what is hidden, to navigate the way together, listening and acting on the promises we make so that "all may see a destiny together."

---

24  Chris Budden, *Following Jesus in Invaded Space: Doing Theology on Aboriginal Land* (Eugene, Oregon: Wipf and Stock, 2009).

# Exposition

Exposition

# 3

# The Call to Transcend Racial Boundaries: An Analysis of the Language in Paragraph 2 of the *Basis of Union*

Joy J. Han

This essay focuses on the following text from paragraph 2 of the *Basis of Union*, especially its notion of "racial boundaries."

> [The Uniting Church] believes that Christians in Australia are called to bear witness to a unity of faith and life in Christ which transcends cultural and economic, national and racial boundaries, and to this end the Uniting Church commits itself to seek special relationships with Churches in Asia and the Pacific.

I take a synchronic view of the above text within the broader context of Australian history. Thus, the historical development of the *Basis* itself does not form the primary context for my exploration, even though it is the source of the text under investigation. Instead I consider more contemporary discourses and initiatives within the Uniting Church in Australia and how they reflect the assumptions and logic of the quoted text. This proceeds from the assumption that Uniting Church language and practices do indeed refer to and reflect the *Basis*.

The first section critically examines certain assumptions in the paragraph 2 excerpt about where racial boundaries actually lie and how they operate. The second section considers how the operation of those same assumptions can be observed in the contemporary life of the Church. Finally, I consider how an intentional re-reading of the quoted text—especially through the hermeneutic of paragraphs 3 and 4—might offer us opportunities to constructively reshape our contemporary proclamations and practices.

Let me also acknowledge before proceeding, that I write as a member of Second Peoples, hoping to redress common biases among Second Peoples and to offer them a perspective that intends to centre First Peoples within the historical context of First Peoples' dispossession. But I am anxious to acknowledge that despite my intentions, my positionality here may operate to render First Peoples invisible if the communication among Second Peoples is taken for granted as the default and centred arena of discourse. Therefore I seek to signal this positionality at various points in the text; however in the words of Gayatri Chakravorty Spivak "I know such gestures can never suffice."[1] I believe that an important component of what can go beyond gestures by Second Peoples is the continued development of perspectives with and in relation to First Peoples and their perspectives, and listening to their distinctive voices.

## Locating the "Racial Boundaries"

We can problematise a number of demarcations found in paragraph 2 by using a postcolonialist lens. For instance, the unqualified use of the term "Australia," and its normative status in the *Basis* as the proper name for the state and its associations gives rise to significant critique from a postcolonialist perspective. As the following paragraphs will argue, it is central to the false construction of racial difference existing beyond rather than within Australian borders. To be sure, such usage is by no means limited to the *Basis*; it reflects wider hegemonic usage. Within the specific context of paragraph 2, however, examining this usage enables us to begin to interpret what the notion of "cultural and economic, national and racial

---

1  Gayatri Chakravorty Spivak, "Can the Subaltern speak?" in *Marxism and the Interpretation of Culture*, ed. Cary Nelson and Lawrence Grossberg (Urbana: University of Illinois Press, 1988), 271.

boundaries" actually entails in the *Basis*. "Australia" is a colonial idea. At best, it disregards or glosses hundreds of distinctive nations of First Peoples whose sovereignty has never been ceded;[2] at worst, it attempts to erase First Peoples. "Australia" is a dispossessive term that both reflects and ideologically perpetuates the unfolding history of dispossession and genocidal violence against First Peoples here.[3] Even if we as Second Peoples are to continue using this term "Australia," and so accept complicity in its violent meaning, we must remain critically aware of its latent aggression. First Peoples – with their languages and critical reflections – continue to offer all of us alternatives to and reappropriations of the idea of "Australia."

Further to its disregard for First Peoples and their history, the language of seeking special relationships with churches in Asia and Pacific as a means to transcending racial boundaries also betrays certain assumptions about who is "Australian." The implication that racial boundaries exist between "Australia" on the one hand and "Asia and the Pacific" on the other perpetuates the myth and phantasy of white Australia. The focus on Asia and the Pacific as a geographic location juxtaposed with Australia overlooks the millennia-old, continuing systems of cultural exchange sustained among First Peoples as well as the presence of Asian and Pasifika

---

2 Cf. The fifteenth Assembly's "affirm[ation] that the First Peoples of Australia, the Aboriginal and Islander Peoples, are sovereign peoples in this land" (Assembly Minute 18.09).

3 For example, Gary Foley writes that "[f]rom the beginning of the British invasion of Australia [I]ndigenous people were slaughtered on a grand scale. In Tasmania between 1804 and 1834, the Aboriginal population was reduced from an estimated 5000 people to just 200, which represented a 90 per cent reduction in just 30 years. In Victoria it has been estimated that the Koori population declined by about 60 per cent in just 15 years between 1835 and 1850 as more than 68 individual 'massacres' were perpetrated in that period." Furthermore, "indiscriminate killings of Aborigines were to continue well into the 1930s." Gary Foley, "Whiteness and Blackness in the Koori Struggle for Self-determination: Strategic Considerations in the Struggle for Social Justice for Indigenous People," *Just Policy*, no. 19-20 (2000): 76-77.

identities within Australia since well before World War Two.[4] Although the received history of immigration in Australia tells the story of progressive opening up after World War Two, this is not the full story. Certainly, there are significant differences between the White Australia Policy and official multiculturalism. But to focus on these differences alone only represents a narrow, white settler-colonial historiography. In the broader context of settler colonialism, the construction of a boundary between "Australia" and "Asia and the Pacific" as a primary racial boundary operates to normalise the notion of Australia as racially homogeneous and originally white. The effect in the text is to alienate First Peoples from their own lands. It also alienates non-white Second Peoples who have the same claim (or lack thereof) as do white settlers to reside here. This privileging of the white settler ultimately serves to legitimate the system and ideology of settler colonialism.

Finally, we can interrogate the implications of paragraph 2's focus on capital-C Churches in Asia and the Pacific. There is in the text the implication that those with whom the Uniting Church will seek special relationships will be institutional Churches, not least those in traditions similar to those of the Uniting Churches. Further, this is suggestive of an assumption that at least some churches in Asia and the Pacific will represent the denominations and structures that find their roots in the European Reformation. This normalises colonial history with its connection to foreign missions from the West to "the Rest." It is true that the movement towards organic union with other Churches as envisioned in paragraph 2 no longer has the currency it once did. In view of that, we can appreciate the historicity of this language and let it rest as such. But there is room to critically reconsider the privileged position that the *Basis* affords the Reformed tradition, at least to the extent that that tradition is understood as having European

---

4 For example, at the time of Federation (1901) there were in fact "substantial numbers of Chinese, Japanese, Indians and Afghans already here." Stuart Macintyre, *A Concise History of Australia*, 3rd ed. (Cambridge: Cambridge University Press, 2009), 144.

origins. This privilege potentiates a Eurocentrism that in turn supports the above mentioned centring of the discourses of white Australia and *terra nullius*.

## Contemporary Dimensions of the Structure of Settler Colonialism

Here are a few examples of how the white-centric and Eurocentric conceits outlined above work themselves out in contemporary discourse in the Uniting Church. These are by no means limited to the language and practice of the Uniting Church, in the same way that the language and assumptions of paragraph 2 are not unique to the *Basis*.

The Uniting Church continues to profess multiculturalism or, specifically, being a multicultural Church as one of its key values. For better or for worse, this is in spite of how the term has been dropped from much of official government policy and more generally has lost its vogue. What is perhaps less appreciated or well-known in the Church's general membership, however, is the postcolonialist critique of multiculturalism that emerged in the 1990s. Not only is there the historiographical criticism that the triumphalism surrounding multiculturalism only makes sense within a narrow national history whose genesis is 1901 and wherein the image of the nation as White Australia is supposedly originary. Certainly the laws constituting the White Australia Policy and their legacies were and are real and devastating, but the notion of Australia as historically white has always been "a falsehood."[5] There is also the criticism that multiculturalism does not comprise a "negation of White ethnocentrism," even though it may appear to do so.[6] Instead, it relies on a differential in agency between white agent and non-white objects to operationalise "an important

---

5  Macintyre, *A Concise History*, 144.
6  Ghassan Hage, *White Nation: Fantasies of White Supremacy in a Multicultural Society* (London: Taylor & Francis Group, 2000), 119.

inherent opposition ... between [white] enriched and [non-white] enriching cultures."[7] Granted, the policy of multiculturalism introduced a qualitative change in the dominant politico-legal imagining of non-white cultures: the change from rejection to proactive valuing.[8] But, as Ghassan Hage's critical examination of how such logics of "valuing" can also be recognised in "various other areas of Australia's social life" shows,[9] multiculturalism does not reconfigure the fundamental structure whereby agency is concentrated in the dominant white culture: "the distinction between valuing negatively/valuing positively mystifies the deeper division between holding the power to value (negatively or positively) and not holding it."[10]

This fundamental structure is that of settler colonialism, parading itself as event and anything but a structure. The ideology of settler colonialism ringfences multiculturalism or matters of "cultural diversity" more generally as a matter focused on non-white, non-black, "ethnic" identities. Thus the culture wars in Australia are bifurcated into matters between black and white peoples on the one hand and multiculturalism on the other.[11] Moreover, both these spheres are marginalised so as to preserve the centre of the political arena for the interests of the white settler.[12]

---

7  Hage, *White Nation*, 118.

8  Hage, *White Nation*, 120-21, 18.

9  Hage, *White Nation*, 119.

10  Hage quotes Heidegger's critique of the discourse of value to note that "[e]very valuing, even when it values positively ... does not let things: be. Rather, valuing lets things: be valid"—with the implication that those things can also be deemed invalid. Heidegger quoted in Hage, *White Nation*, 121.

11  Or, as Hage would call it: "white multiculturalism".

12  It is within this analysis that we can critically survey the contemporary framing of asylum seeker and refugee matters as primarily a humanitarian concern in terms of a European human rights framework, without regard for their continuity with the humanitarian crisis that comprises the frontier wars and their ongoing legacies, including but not limited to the overrepresentation of Indigenous Australians in the criminal justice system.

A natural correlate of multiculturalism and its valuing logics is the commodification of culture. Commodifying logics, as Hage explains, are evident in rhetoric such as that of "productive diversity," a federal government policy component during Paul Keating's prime ministership (1991–96) which sought to mobilise an "exploitation of ethnicity to make it yield a kind of ethnic surplus value."[13] In a capitalist economy, the more value the better, which fosters a competitive environment wherein participants in the "marketplace of cultures" are incentivised to advertise, through various performative means, their own cultural scarcity and distinctiveness over others'. In the life of the Uniting Church, the risks identified by this analysis are perhaps most apparent in the largely siloed structuring of the National Conferences that "provide opportunities for people of the same culture to meet together for worship, fellowship and development."[14]

Meanwhile, a more longitudinal view highlights anxieties more deep-seated than those generated by free market economics. In a context where First Peoples continue to struggle for others' recognition of their being and their bloodshed, nobody is culturally safe. Appeals to one's cultural endangerment and distinctiveness are not just performative; they are also a plea for survival. Even the dominant culture must mobilise an elaborate ideological state apparatus to assert and sustain its hegemony. In an atmosphere where culture is valued but never "underwritten", so to speak, ethnobiological exogamy tends to be pathologised. This in turn leads to a fixation on so-called "second-generation" or "next-gen" — even "1.5-gen"[15]—migrants who are assessed for their "value"

---

13  Hage, *White Nation*, 129.

14  "National Conferences," Uniting Church in Australia, accessed March 1, 2022, https://assembly.uca.org.au/mcm/resources/other-resources/item/1005-about-national-conferences.

15  For further discussion of the operation of the language of the "three-generations hypothesis" in the context of the Uniting Church, see Joy J. Han, "Second-generation Migrant Bodies: Site of Ideological Reproduction and Implications for the Body of Christ," in *Bordered Bodies, Bothered Voices: Native and Local Theologies*, ed. Jione Havea (Eugene: Wipf and Stock, 2022), 145.

on the basis of their capacity to take on the baton of lived and performative cultural distinctiveness and rarity. Simply put, youth and young adults who fall short of the ideal of the ethnically "pure" phenotype who is proficient in the mother tongue, and heteronormatively endogamous and reproductive (not to mention able-bodied) are prone to be undervalued by the Church community's dominant discourse.[16]

At a fundamental philosophical level, the Western and Eurocentric commodifying and essentialising logics outlined above are animated by Platonic accounts of identity and difference. The notion of identity as we know it is predicated upon Platonic Ideas as stable points of reference, while difference is reduced to the mere "negative space" between proper-noun identities. The Platonic legacy lacks a positive or cataphatic account of difference. Continental philosophy, notably the work of Gilles Deleuze, has contributed to critiques of how Platonism is inadequate in its explanation of how identities (other than those of, say, mathematical entities or chemical elements) evolve over time.[17] A fuller exploration of the relevant history of philosophy is beyond the scope of this chapter. Suffice to say that the Western overreliance on this historically specific account of identity and difference presents us with roadblocks as we seek to embody and theologically reflect upon diversity in the community. In particular, the increasing entrenchment in Uniting Church discourse of the ecclesial trinity of "Anglo," "Congress" and "Culturally and Linguistically Diverse" as supposedly mutually exclusive and

---

16  The risks that such idealisation poses to young people in terms of both sexual ethics (e.g. heteronormatively endogamous and reproductive pressures) and Safe Church (e.g. idealised young leaders who may come into an excess of power over children or other vulnerable persons) warrant further investigation as a matter of priority.

17  See for instance Gilles Deleuze, *Difference and Repetition [Différence et Répétition]*, trans. Paul Patton (New York: Bloomsbury Publishing, 2010), 1

collectively exhaustive hypostases is overdue for critical reassessment.[18] Reductionist ontological essentialism only mires us in tokenistic body count politics at the expense of deeper dialogue that both acknowledges and pushes the limits of multiple, coexisting epistemological paradigms. Covenanting and Walking Together as First and Second Peoples are discourses that afford us opportunities to intentionally reveal rather than conceal the truth about race relations and justice for First Peoples. They move us beyond euphemistic racial profiling, so that people are better positioned to speak for themselves, rather than as a representative of some undifferentiated, homogeneous mass known by the name of an ethnic, racial or other marker.

## A Gospel of Relocated and Reimagined Racial Boundaries

In view of the specific challenges catalogued above this section identifies some opportunities to critically reappropriate the assumptions and omissions of the language of paragraph 2, particularly through the lens of paragraphs 3 and 4.

Most pressing is the imperative to disrupt the self-perpetuating falsehoods of white settler colonialism. Practically speaking, the realisation that settler colonialism is, as Patrick Wolfe argues, a structure and not an event may facilitate greater recognition by more Second Peoples of the fact that nobody on stolen land can remain indifferent to the violence of settler colonialism.[19] We

---

18 The term "CALD," like "Australia," is at once attempted erasure of First Nations and a pandering to white exceptionalism, as though non-white Second Peoples were the only groups with "culture" and "language." Of course the usage reflects the reality that Second Peoples' are the only "cultures" and "languages" that the white centre openly commodifies. Certainly First Nations' cultural artefacts are all too readily commodified as well—or rather stolen, since the dominant ideology must take care not to tip the balance into proper recognition or acknowledgment of First Peoples and their continuing cultures.

19 On Wolfe's distinction between structure and event, see Patrick Wolfe, *Settler Colonialism and the Transformation of Anthropology: The Politics and Poetics of an Ethnographic Event* (London: Bloomsbury, 1998), 2.

must confess with historical particularity the ways in which the "new order of righteousness and love" (BOU, 3) brings justice and healing in the face of the old order. By all means, the call to "bear witness to a unity of faith and life in Christ which transcends ... racial boundaries" is one fulfilled abroad. But the same call is heard here on country—on stolen yet never ceded lands and waters—each and every day. The indwelling sin of the myth of *terra nullius* is due to be met with sustained efforts to proclaim Christ as Lord against the tyranny and trauma of history. It is the specific unfolding of settler colonialism (among other dimensions of history) through which "the Church is able to live and endure ... only because its Lord comes, addresses, and deals with people in and through the news of his completed work" (BOU, 4). The gospel must directly proclaim repentance for Second Peoples from the guilt of and complicity with colonial and epistemic violence—not by fiat, but through an embodied process in relationship with and led by First Peoples. The resurrection too must speak directly to the restoration of lost lives, languages and sacred sites; and healing for the trauma that affects all peoples living under settler colonialism.

A gospel proclamation that is contextualised within the structure of settler colonialism entails a key prerequisite: namely, the proper recognition of the immediacy of settler colonialism and its devastating impacts. If paragraph 2 is blind to the entrenchment of racial boundaries within what is called "Australia," then this ought to serve as a warning that as a community the dominant discourse of the Church is systemically biased so as to silence the voices that name and declaim those racial boundaries and their effects. As this paper has sought to demonstrate, the presently dominant discourse fails to recognise the ways in which racial boundaries keep our community divided and estranged. Indeed this problem affects discourse at large, not just Church conversations. This poses challenges and opportunities for our dominant liturgies. Our Church must not be satisfied to perform multilingual worship services with colourful song and dance as evidence of our having transcended boundaries. We are called to make public (cf. *leitourgia*) the end of settler colonialism, cultural commodification and casual racism. Testimony regarding intergenerational and embodied trauma must be honoured—in and of itself, but also as a chance to acknowledge, and educate the wider community about, experiences that are not always readily validated by conventional or academic discourse. Without due space for such *parrhesia* we cannot expect to hear or recognise testimony regarding the healing to follow. Meanwhile, Indigenous Australian theologies and contextual theologies must not be offered up for consumption as exotic delicacies. They engage us dynamically as evolving lines of enquiry that can and must decentre the dominance of Eurocentric theological and liturgical traditions in the Church.

The language found in paragraph 3 of "a body within which the diverse gifts of its members are used for the building up of the whole" need not roll up into the valuing logics criticised earlier. Members themselves are not "gifts" but rather receive gifts. Therefore dominant cultural identities must not confuse "being diverse" as something embodied by other people on the margins who in turn are "received" by people in the centre as a gift. Proper attention to the language presents us with opportunities to relocate the lines of diversity not among, say, Anglo, Congress and CALD, but instead diachronically – across the continuing history of the Church. For example, Covenanting and the functions of prophecy, theological reflection, administration and more that spearhead it are "diverse gifts" that build up the whole. The mere fact or "body count" of diversity does not constitute an "instrument through which Christ may work and bear witness to himself" (BOU, 3). Rather, it is how we engage in the fellowship of the Holy Spirit with one another in and through that dynamic diversity.

The exploration of multiple cultural and ethnic identities within and across the most obvious racial categories provides hope for those who do not readily fit those racial profiles to be heard for who they are. The celebrated Uniting Church principle of council members speaking for themselves and not their appointing body is all the more pertinent when it comes to hearing individuals to whom settler colonialism has appointed roughshod racial profiles.

## Concluding Remarks

Further critical reflection on our language for "cultural and economic, national and racial boundaries" is long overdue. This has been a number of observations from just one person's perspective, offering analyses that attempt to place a critique of settler colonialism at the focal point of a postcolonialist lens. Although I have criticised the assumptions that underlie the language of paragraph 2, this is by no means intended to write off the text as outmoded or poisoned. The silences and omissions in the text have a negative presence that we can appropriate and bring to our critical awareness in the spirit of self-examination.

# 4

# Tradition in the *Basis of Union*: Silences, Exclusions and Openings

Liam Miller

## Introduction

'Tongues' were lost; mother tongues were buried while human tongues were cut from mouths. Women's tongues were silenced for centuries. What survived entered into a covenant of silence, and since then it has never fully spoken again.

Marcella Althaus-Reid.[1]

Marcella Althaus-Reid (1952-2009) argues that the Grand Narratives of the original nations and Indigenous peoples of Latin America collapsed under the authoritarian process of conquest and colonisation. The people "were brutalised into Christian Grand Narratives" with the "Great European Meta-narratives" being imposed on their lives.[2] The authority establishing itself in this process (which is shared with "western theological authority") is composed of a "modern conception of (Western) linear time" and a "core knowledge base provided by the construction of the Western subject as constitutive of the real."[3] In this process of conquest and exploitation Christianity was offered as a righteous replacement for Indigenous wickedness. As Thia Cooper summarises, "salvation was exchanged for submission," meaning "the Cacique could only receive grace by giving up all his previous knowledge and

---

1 Marcella Althaus-Reid, *Indecent Theology* (London: Routledge, 2000), 11.
2 Althaus-Reid, *Indecent Theology*, 12.
3 Althaus-Reid, *Indecent Theology*, 13.

culture."[4] This system, where salvation was available only through the religion of the coloniser, meant the Indigenous were reliant on God's grace and the colonist's tradition. The result of this exchange is the establishment of a theological economy where, in the words of Althaus-Reid, the Indigenous "do not own theology, they just rent it."[5] This arrangement is typical of what Althaus-Reid calls T-Theology, "a totalitarian construction of what is considered 'The One and Only Theology' which does not admit discussions or challenges from different perspectives"[6] and "seldom lets us perceive the historical presence of God in different, unfamiliar surroundings."[7]

While the colonial violence and establishment of Western authority and narrative on these lands is distinct from that which occurred in Latin America, there are connections between what Althaus-Reid is observing and what has been documented in this place. Garry Worete Deverell has written that the passing on of lore

> is precisely the process which colonisers sought to disrupt. For they knew that the very survival of Aboriginal and Torres Strait Islander peoples as Aboriginal and Torres Strait Islander peoples depends on it. That is why they removed us from country, separated us from elders, and forbade us to speak or sing or otherwise perform our language and lore. They wanted to remove us from our dreaming and kill our spirit. But that is easier said than done![8]

The disruption and denial of this lore is part and parcel of the imposition of a new, Western grand narrative, one which has nothing to gain from those it is subjugating. It is the assertion of a Tradition over and against, and to the exclusion of all

---

4 Thia Cooper, *Queer and Indecent* (London: SCM Press, 2021), 51.
5 Cooper, *Queer and Indecent*, 52.
6 Marcella Althaus-Reid, *The Queer God* (London: Routledge, 2003), 174.
7 Althaus-Reid, *Queer God*, 33.
8 Garry Worete Deverell, *Gondwana Theology* (Victoria: Morning Star Publishing, 2018), 16.

others. The tradition, of course, can only be wielded in such a way, when it is assumed to be in the possession of those who name it. As Aileen Moreton-Robinson demonstrates, "knowledge and power are produced in and through concepts in relation to possession. You cannot dominate without seeking to possess the dominated. You cannot exclude unless you assume you already own."[9] The possessive quality of whiteness perceives as threat ways of Indigenous knowing and claims to Indigenous sovereignty. The nation, like the tradition, already has an owner. The assertion of sovereign authority and knowledge from a non-western subject outside of the authorising systems of whiteness, is met with suspicion. To note one example, in her recent work, *Another Day in the Colony*, Chelsea Watego exposes the ongoing "unease of colleagues and students" grappling with the idea that she "exist authentically as knower and 'native' at one time."[10] The Indigenous writer, Watego observes, "is permitted to feel, but not think" and that "in their written testimony [they] can only ever authorise and accessorise coloniser mythologies – they can never theorise their existence. Well, mostly."[11] There is, to summarise, an assumption at play on who is allowed to know, and who can rent (so long as they meet the conditions of the knower). And because of this there is the silencing of the accounts and language of those not found in the Western subject and lineage.

With these considerations in hand, I will take this anniversary engagement with the *Basis of Union* as an opportunity to ask whether the *Basis* perpetuates the kind of silencing, the kind of authoritative imposition of the Western theological lineage and subject as constitutive of the real, while perceiving the rest as life-long renters? Is the *Basis* another case of theological utterance, which, in the words of Deverell "continues to pretend that none of

---

9  Aileen Moreton-Robinson, *The White Possessive* (Minneapolis: University of Minnesota Press, 2015), xxiv.

10  Chelsea Watego, *Another Day in the Colony* (Queensland: University of Queensland Press, 2021), 10.

11  Watego, *Another Day*, 56.

this has happened, that the vocation of Australian theology need be nothing other than a positively framed elaboration of steadfastly European concerns and themes."[12]

An argument could be developed that this is the case. To the extent that this tradition is identified and explicitly named in the *Basis*, it is a decidedly Western product. The various creeds, catechisms, confessions and sermons all come to these lands from the West (and North), and from the lineage and ancestry of the uniting churches. Further, the progression of the *Basis* (beginning with the coming of Christ, and then proceeding through the formation of the church, gifting of scripture and sacrament, to the creeds and reformation witness) could be read as suggesting a linear path of historical progress where the Western tradition is essential to the One and Only narrative of theological unfolding wherein Christianity must come (to any latecomers) through Rome and Europe. If the *Basis* is read in this linear framework, then are we a church that declares itself multicultural and intercultural despite a monocultural tradition, that recognises Indigenous sovereignty while silencing Indigenous voices, that places Jesus' pivotal question on his identity within the bounds of the language and judgments of a time and place far away from here?

The stakes are high. And while it would be a folly to approach the *Basis* as a document that somehow dodged the colonial mindset and trappings, in wrestling with these questions I will show that the *Basis* has openings that foster a particular posture toward the explicitly named tradition. This posture can resist a One and Only narrative, resist the western subject as constitutive of the real, and replace silence with cacophony of theological expression in many tongues.

To work toward this hope I argue that the language utilised in paragraphs 9 and 10 of the *Basis* (where this Tradition is considered) depart significantly from that which has gone before. This shift, which is evident in the change of active agent (from

---

12 Deverell, *Gondwana Theology*, 22.

Christ to the church) and in the various verbs that convey how the tradition is entered into and used, opens the door for a critical and constructive relationship with this tradition. Indeed, as we will see, the language chosen for paragraphs 9 and 10 resembles far more that of paragraph 11 (and its considerations of contemporary interpretation and wisdom) than what precedes. This distinction provides opening for the church to negotiate particular postures towards the tradition so it may be ready when occasion demands to confess the Lord in fresh words and deeds.

## The Priority and Initiative of God in the Language of Paragraphs 3-8

In now turning to the *Basis*, I will proceed by working through paragraphs 3-8. Throughout these paragraphs, God (or God in Christ who in turn actions the Holy Spirit) is the instigating and acting agent. "God in Christ has given to all people in the Church the Holy Spirit" (BOU, 3), "Christ feeds the church with word and sacrament ..." (BOU, 3), "Christ reaches out to command people's attention ... he calls people" (BOU, 4), "[Christ] comes, addresses, and deals with people" (BOU, 4). "Christ himself acts in and through everything that the Church does", Christ confers forgiveness, fellowship and freedom, "Christ awakens, purifies and advances" (BOU, 6). "Christ incorporates" (BOU, 7), "the risen Lord feeds" (BOU, 8). Give, feed, reach, command, call, addresses, deals, confers, awakens, purifies, advances, incorporates ... a series of active verbs where Christ is the subject and the church the object being acted upon.

Understandably, the posture of the church is decidedly more passive. Evidenced immediately in how each of these paragraphs begin: "The Uniting Church acknowledges..." To acknowledge is not an interpretive act, rather it is an admission of reality, existence, truth. Taking the analogy of the acknowledgment of country: the one doing the acknowledgment performs nothing, casts nothing into being, but simply admits or notes a reality within which they exist.

Other than acknowledging, the church "confesses Jesus as Lord... [and] Head over all things" (BOU, 3). The church "has received the books of the Old and New Testaments ... in which it hears the Word of God ... by which its faith and obedience are nourished and regulated" and its "message is controlled" (BOU, 5). Acknowledge, confess, receive, is nourished, regulated, controlled; a stark contrast from the activity of Christ. The responsibility of the church toward Christ, as well as that which mediates or conveys the reality of Christ's achievement to us, is to properly posture itself toward a reality hurtling toward it. There is a strong consistency across paragraphs 3-8, whereby Christ is the primary character and the subject of the most active verbs, whereas the church takes a passive role; acknowledging a completed work that breaks in upon us today and being fed and formed by a reality beyond our control.

## The Activity and Agency of the Church in the Language of Paragraphs 9-10

We come now to paragraphs 9 and 10, which concern the creeds and the reformation witness. To start, the phrase "The Uniting Church acknowledges" is jettisoned in favour of: "enters into unity with the Church ..." (BOU, 9) in the case of the Creeds and "continues to learn..." (BOU, 10) in the case of the Reformation Witness. This is an immediate shift to more complex language, that grants the church more agency than anything we've seen thus far, a shift that continues to frame the paragraphs.

*Paragraph 9*

Starting with the creeds, the entry into unity is via the church's "use" of these confessions, a verb that keeps the church as the subject that acts upon an object. It is also important to note that the creeds are not established on their own, they are by-product, or way in, to a broader idea: "unity with the Church throughout the ages." The *Basis* does speak of the church as receiving the creeds, yet they are not afforded the same potency as the Scriptures where "received" is also used.

What we receive from the creeds is their status as much as – if not more than – their content. They are "authoritative statements of the Catholic Faith" that are "framed in the language of their day" and used – again language pointing to the value in utility rather than a reality in se – for a specific purpose: "to declare and to guard the right understanding of that faith" – note again, the qualifier "that" rather than "the" or "our" faith. The *Basis* receives these creeds because of the particular role they have played within the Church and because that role is one that allows us – by also using them – to enter into unity with that Church. There is nothing stated about the role of Christ or the Spirit in the production, bestowing, or givenness of these documents, and nothing about the content of the documents as compelling or forming the Uniting Church and its confession.

The emphasis on the human subject continues when considering exactly how the creeds are said to be used: "The Uniting Church commits its ministers and instructors to careful study of these creeds and to the discipline of interpreting their teaching in a later age." Compared to the serious duty of reading Scripture that is laid upon all members, it is only ministers and instructors within the church who are called to study the creeds and to engage a discipline of interpreting them in a later age. This is the second of two occasions in this paragraph where the gulf between the then of the creeds and the now of now is noted. There is a commending of the creeds to congregations, but again, it is for specific purposes, and the minister and congregation retain the position of acting subject: "use for instruction" and "use in worship as acts of allegiance to the Holy Trinity." Again, nothing is said about how the Holy Trinity might use, be present in, or bestow the creed. They are statements of the faith that, though framed in the language of their day can, through interpretation, be used to serve various purposes.

## Paragraph 10

The paragraph on the Reformation witnesses carries a similar tone. The various confessions, catechisms, and declarations that express the witness of the Reformers is presented as something we may use to continue our learning of the Holy Scriptures. The Scriptures are the point, and the Reformation witness is suitable in so far as it reminds us of the grace which justifies through faith, the centrality of the person and work of Christ, and the need for a constant appeal to Holy Scripture. There is an interpretive act already in play in this paragraph, the Reformation witness and Wesley's sermons are not a good in and of themselves (or at least not commended as a thing themselves). They are handed on, in the trust that from them – again via our efforts of study and interpretation – we might be reminded of some already held beliefs. Again, this paragraph does not contain any references to God, Jesus, or Holy Spirit as acting subjects (perhaps with the small exception of the reference to the promised gift of the Holy Spirit, but again, that promise is about the possibility of our right reading, rather than attached to the reformers writings).

Paragraphs 9 and 10 take a stark departure from that which precedes. The activity of the Triune God moves into the background, foregrounding instead the interpretive action of the church, and its use of various documents from the tradition. The language around these documents is more open and passive. The documents are rarely spoken of in themselves (or in terms of their content); instead the attention is on the way they have been and can possibly be used either to draw us into unity with the church, remind us of truths found in scripture, or support our allegiance to and worship of God.

## The Mixed Affair of Paragraph 11

The language of paragraph 11 is a more mixed affair. It returns to acknowledging the activity of God: who "has never left the Church without faithful and scholarly interpreters of Scripture those who reflect deeply on God's living Word ..." Compared to the creeds which are framed as a product of the church, this reflection is a product of God's fidelity. Yet, there are similarities to paragraphs 9 and 10. The church takes on the role of active subject as it "enters into the inheritance of literary, historical and scientific enquiry," and again, like the content of 9 and 10, this inheritance is engaged insofar as it opens itself to the knowledge of God's ways via our interpretive efforts.

But then, in language distinct from 9 and 10, paragraph 11 gives thanks to God "for the continuing witness and service of evangelist, of scholar, of prophet and of martyr," and then – in the more pious language that has emerged in this paragraph – the Uniting Church "prays that it may be ready when occasion demands to confess the Lord in fresh words and deeds." Fresh words and deeds here potentially playing as a counterweight to the creeds in the language of their day. To summarise, paragraph 11 aligns with paragraphs 3-8 in its acknowledgment of God as the active subject and shares with 9 and 10 the focus on the church and its interpretive efforts to use the inheritance to draw us to knowledge of God.

If we were thinking in segments, paragraphs 9 and 10 belong much more with 11 than with 3-8, and 11 seems to hold more potency. Paragraphs 9 and 10 stress the need for interpretive efforts on the part of ministers and instructors to both move backward through the creeds and reformation witness to the truths found in scripture and forward to their proper use in the ecclesial setting. On the other hand, paragraph 11, declares the importance of the contemporary sources and witness as contributing to nothing less than our ability to confess the Lord in fresh words and deeds, which is, in many ways, the vocation of the disciple. With this analysis in mind, I want to offer some concluding thoughts on the posture of the *Basis* toward the Tradition as well as some opening thoughts on how the *Basis* might move us towards that which stands outside of such a Tradition.

## Some Concluding Openings

There is a silencing at work in the *Basis*. Unlike the later Preamble to the Constitution there is no named acknowledgment of the particular theological knowledge of Indigenous peoples, nor the activity of God in law, custom, and ceremony. There are no explicit references to expressions of faith developed and developing in Asia and Pasifika. Indeed, where the tradition is named, it reflects and is contained in a Western, patriarchal church. And yet, the *Basis* also deflates overly enthusiastic attempts to align this tradition with a single lineage of God's activity. The *Basis* places distance between the activity of God and the Creeds/Reformation witness, while placing greater emphasis on God's activity in the work and witness of contemporary interpreters and disciples.

Further, there are openings in the *Basis* where the power and presence of the risen Christ can be read to push against the authority of modern Western linear time. Paragraphs 3-8 are ripe with the present tense-ness of Christ's activity, who brings that which has happened into a happening. Similarly, paragraph 11 reminds us of God's present and ongoing faithfulness that is responsible for the contemporary inheritance and learning the church enters into. The only paragraphs stuck in time are 9 and 10, where the creeds and reformation witness are acknowledged to be of their day. By this, the *Basis* might be said to hold within it potential to resist a particular western, progressive/developmental concept of history (where all roads run through Nicaea and Europe). This opens up a posture that does not require the privileging of what came before simply because it came before.

Returning to the conversations and question that started this paper, I contend that the test of whether the *Basis* performs an act of white possession by silencing voices beyond the Tradition, or instead makes room for a cacophony of confessing tongues, is how wide, surprising, and indecent we are willing to read paragraph 11. How many people and communities are able to be found in its categories? Are we ready, with Althaus-Reid to "perceive the historical presence of God in different, unfamiliar surroundings"? And what agency and authority will be afforded their witness as they testify to the faith even as it disrupts and upends the settled assumptions not only of paragraphs 9 and 10, but the whole *Basis* and more!

Here, the anachronistic (but commonly included) paragraph title of "scholarly interpreters" lends a disservice to our approach. If the definition and limit of those who have faithfully interpreted scripture and deeply reflected on God's word are limited to those who have studied within the institutions and reading lists of the Tradition, then paragraph 11 will be of little help. Any hope of the *Basis* resisting its colonial trappings needs to be led by a multiplicity of those not only at the margins, but off the maps of those who enshrined the Tradition.

Hence it is helpful to open up paragraph 11 with Marcella Althaus-Reid. Althaus-Reid sought to displace the One and Only narrative of capital T-Theology so that – through upending assumptions of normativity via engagement with the lived experiences of those often ignored and marginalised (and the fullness of their religious, sexual, economic lives at that) – we would be able to celebrate the diverse ways of knowing God. Indeed, God would be able to come out of the closet of the tradition serving a reminder that God is not a God of the centre but the margins.[13]

Althaus-Reid is careful to delineate between a central God who is "an occasional and compassionate visitor to the margins" and "a truly marginal God... who has never left the margins."[14] A central God is created by the centres of the world for their own ends. This

---

13  Cooper, *Queer and Indecent*, 140, 141.
14  Marcella Althaus-Reid, *From Feminist Theology to Indecent Theology* (London: SCM Press, 2004), 146.

God is easily able to move to the margins without falling off the "master's map" because the "centre nurtures its epistemology."[15] God remains possessed and unchanged and the hope is to develop the margins into line with the centre. Yet "margins are not margins, but geographies in their own right"[16] and need to be allowed to act as "unauthorised sites of divinity" that upend the tradition and expand conceptions of God.[17] As Cooper summarises: "God expands beyond God's limits at the margins" pulled away from the false centre "becoming a larger God ... This God is in movement, expanding and loving."[18]

In the case of the *Basis*, we might frame this distinction thusly (drawing here on Watego): are those on the margins only allowed to theologise in ways that authorise and accessorise what has already been enshrined as the Tradition, or can they stand on their own ground and authority as one who God has seen, upending and expanding theology? The driving assumption of Althaus-Reid is that the poor and untouchable in society have already experienced and are experiencing God, already live with God in a vital and intimate way. To honour this, Althaus-Reid argued that "Sometime theology should declare an independence day, and start anew, from the real grassroots of marginal communities."[19]

Not that anyone in these communities is necessarily asking for such a "permission", but I contend that the *Basis of Union*'s acknowledgment of God's gift to the church of those "who have reflected deeply upon, and acted trustingly in obedience to, God's living Word" is an opening to such an upending, to such a quest into new geographies, to such a relinquishing of fallacies of

---

15  Marcella Althaus-Reid, "The Divine Exodus of God: Involuntarily Marginalized, Taking an Option for the Margins, or Truly Marginal?" in *God, Experience and Mystery* ed. W.G Jeanrond and C. Theobold (London: SCM Press, 2001), 31

16  Althaus-Reid, "Divine Exodus," 32.

17  Althaus-Reid, "Divine Exodus," 31.

18  Cooper, *Queer and Indecent*, 138-139.

19  Althaus-Reid, "Divine Exodus," 32.

possession, to such an independence day where many tongues long silenced may teach the whole church how to confess the Lord in fresh words and deeds.

# 5

# Bound and Free: The Legacy of
# the *Basis of Union* for Ordination[1]

## Michael Earl

## Introduction

Ordination has been a topic that has invited much debate, reflection and conversation in the life of the Uniting Church. It has been the subject of numerous formal statements,[2] repetitive and wearying discussions across councils,[3] and a persistent point of contention in ecumenical dialogue.[4] This reflects a widely unsettled internal culture. As the church marks the fiftieth anniversary of the *Basis of Union* its founding theological statement, it is an appropriate time for reflection on this critical and conflicted aspect of its life. This paper will do so by addressing the tension

---

1 The title, "Bound and Free" is borrowed from the theological memoir of North American Protestant theologian Douglas John Hall, *Bound and Free: A Theologian's Journey* (Minneapolis, Fortress Press: 2005), though its lineage goes back much further.

2 Stephen Burns notes that in Rob Bos and Geoff Thompson's "valuable collection" of important documents from the UCA's formal conversations (*Theology for Pilgrims*), reports on ordination/ministry 'occupy well over half of the anthology's pages – itself an indication of unsettled and contested thinking in this area within the Uniting Church.' Stephen Burns, "'Limping Priests' Ten Years Later: Formation for Ordained Ministry," *Uniting Church Studies* 17, no. 2 (December 2011): 3.

3 Graham Hughes notes that, "the most recent inquiry on ordination undertaken by our church names itself as the seventh such detailed statement since 1963." And more have followed (2004, 2008). Graham Hughes, "Limping Priests: ministry and ordination," *Uniting Church Studies* 8, no. 1 (March 2002): 1.

4 See Christiaan Mostert, "Church, Ministry, and Ordination: What Relation?" *Uniting Church Studies* 10, no. 1 (March 2004): 20-30.

embedded in the *Basis*: the "boundedness" inherent in ordination and the "freedom" to explore flexible forms of ministry.

## The Ambiguity of Paragraph 14

In a tone of lament in 1997, inaugural President Davis McCaughey wrote, "The most substantial thing that concerns me about the life of the Uniting Church: [is] the arbitrary attitude adopted so frequently to the doctrine of [ordained] ministry."[5] This is a significant statement considering the range issues with which the UCA had grappled to this point in its history. The church's oscillations on ordination have been widely cited. Graham Hughes observed the 'deep restlessness and uncertainty in the church about the practice of ordination.[6] Val Webb questioned, "Is it permissible to ask why we ordain at all?"[7] Anita Monro asserted that there is a need for "reclaiming the ordered ministry of the Word in the Uniting Church."[8] Stephen Burns wrote of the "long conflict and ... confusion about ministry in the Uniting Church."[9]

Combined with a typically Australian pragmatism often evident in UCA discussions of ministry, the "arbitrary" attitude McCaughey lamented has ensured that ordination has remained

5  J Davis McCaughey, "If I Had Known Then What I Know Now," in *Marking Twenty Years: The Uniting Church in Australia 1977-1997*, eds. William & Susan Emilsen (North Parramatta: United Theological College Publications, 1997), 7.

6  Graham Hughes, "Limping Priests," 1.

7  Val Webb, "Is It Permissible to Ask Why We Ordain at All?", *Uniting Church Studies* 3, no. 1, (March 1997): 13.

8  Anita Monro, "It's such a shame you're not in a congregation!" Reclaiming the Ordered Ministry of the Word in the Uniting Church," *Uniting Church Studies* 21, no. 1, (June 2017): 31.

9  Stephen Burns, "Ministry," in *An Informed Faith: The Uniting Church at the Beginning of the 21st Century*, ed. William Emilsen (Melbourne: Morning Star Publications, 2014), 39.

confused and contested ground in the UCA.[10] Hughes identified a range of wider cultural factors that have contributed to so febrile an environment,[11] but the seeds for ferment were sown into the *Basis of Union* itself in Paragraph 14. McCaughey averred in 1980 that "[f]ew words in the Basis have caused as much trouble since union as those with which Paragraph 14 ends."[12] After offering a recognisably Reformed/Evangelical statement on the "ministry of the Word," and a detailed description of the rite itself (section 'a'),[13] those troublesome "few words" are these found in section 'd':

> The Uniting Church recognises that the type and duration of ministries to which women and men are called vary from time to time and place to place, and that in particular it comes into being in a period of reconsideration of traditional forms of the ministry, and of a renewed participation of all the people of God in the preaching of the Word, the administration of the sacraments, the building up of the fellowship in mutual love, in commitment to Christ's mission, and in service of the world for which he died. (BOU, 14d)

This is a particularly loaded statement for a uniting communion made up of three distinct traditions, for which ordination had already been a contentious matter prior to union, necessitating a redrafting of this paragraph prior to the church's vote on the

10 This is not to say considered, thoughtful theological work has not been forthcoming, indeed the formal reports of 1991 (*Ministry in the Uniting Church*) and 1994 (*Ordination and Ministry in the Uniting Church*) both represent careful appropriations of the Reformed/Evangelical tradition's ordination theology. Both can be found in Rob Bos and Geoff Thompson, eds. *Theology for Pilgrims: Selected Theological Documents of the Uniting Church in Australia* (Sydney: Uniting Church Press, 2008).

11 Graham Hughes, "Limping Priests," 1-4.

12 J Davis McCaughey, *Commentary on the Basis of Union* (Melbourne: Uniting Church Press, 1980), 83.

13 Further underlining its significance for the life of the church and a concern for faithful transmission of the Reformed/Evangelical tradition's understanding in the minds of the drafters of the *Basis of Union*.

*Basis*.[14] Earlier on the *Basis of Union* had stated with conventional Reformed/Evangelical emphases: "the Church ... will ... call and set apart members ... to be ministers of the Word" (BOU, 14a)[15] and that "these will preach the Gospel, administer the sacraments and exercise pastoral care so that all may be equipped for their particular ministries, thus maintaining the apostolic witness to Christ in the Church ... and their setting apart ... known as Ordination" (BOU, 14a). But the final statement appears to problematise those very commitments.

Especially ambiguous is the fraught suggestion of "reconsideration of traditional forms of the ministry"(BOU, 14).[16] On the face of it, this could mean either reconsidering how the "traditional forms" are understood and practised, or, more radically, questioning their very existence. For the drafters' part, clearly the former is intended. As McCaughey insists, "[these words] cannot be interpreted as a denial of what is asserted so clearly elsewhere that preaching and the administration of the sacraments are the special responsibility of ministers of the Word."[17] Even with this clarification, the words remain ambiguous and open to interpretation.

Additional issues arise. It is far from clear how these "few words" sit with the overt ecumenical aspirations of the UCA. Nor is it clear what they might signify in a church whose own cultural diversity has exposed the connections between ordination,

---

14  See J Davis McCaughey, *The Basis of Union: A Commentary*, ed. Andrew Dutney (Sydney: National Assembly of the Uniting Church, 2016), 28-30. Note that this is a separate work from McCaughey's 1980 commentary already referenced. See also D'Arcy Wood, *Building on a Solid Basis: A Guide to the Basis of Union*, (Melbourne: Uniting Church Press, 1986) 44.

15  'Of Word and Sacrament' in some traditions – McCaughey noted in 1997 that he felt it had been a 'mistake' not to use the 'full phrase' in the *Basis*, see "If I Had Known Then What I Know Now," 8.

16  The definite article seems to suggest it is especially (only?) ordained ministry that is in mind here. Perhaps much controversy could have been avoided simply by dropping the definite article and so broadening the focus of what was in view for "reconsideration."

17  J Davis McCaughey, *Commentary* (1980), 82.

authority and cultural heritage. It is also readily exploitable by the Australian tendency to be suspicious of a conferred authority. Questions abound.

So, what is the point of these "few words"? McCaughey writes that the intention is to shift away from the view that makes the laity "passive" recipients of the Word.[18] Such a stance is reflective of the prevailing mood of the time in which the whole people of God were being re-centred as the theologically appropriate, primary locus of ministry,[19] recognising that it is, as Burns writes, in the first place a "baptismal category."[20] The impression left by the concluding words of Paragraph 14, however, can feel less like an encouragement out of passivity for the laity and more like an undermining of the proper place of ordained ministry. Either way, it clearly contributed to an already contested environment, creating further confusion.

Ironically, these "few words" also potentially confuse the true nature of lay ministry as the Reformed/Evangelical tradition has understood it. "Lay" ministry is supposed to work in a complementary, interdependent partnership with ordained ministry, not to displace it.[21] By linking the "renewed participation" of the laity with the three-fold tasks of preaching, presiding and pastoring

---

18  J Davis McCaughey, *Commentary* (1980), 82.

19  The World Council of Churches, Faith and Order Paper No. 111, *Baptism, Eucharist, and Ministry* (Geneva: WCC, 1982), is the most significant ecumenical statement of the time, one to which many churches including the UCA made a considered response, and which, like the *Basis*, locates ministry in the first place as a calling of all the baptised, hence the ordering with Baptism first and Ministry last.

20  Stephen Burns, "Ministry," 37. That is, not the purview wholly of the ordained. This position is stated in unequivocal terms in Paragraph 13.

21  'Lay' used here in its narrow sense in order to differentiate from 'ordained', not in its broader sense to mean 'all the people of God' who live and serve under the Word. On interdependence of ordained/lay, see J Davis McCaughey, *Commentary on the Basis of Union* (1980), 82 and D'Arcy Wood, *Building on a Solid Basis: A Guide to the Basis of Union*, 48-49.

as the particular charge of the ordained, important and proper lines of distinction are again significantly blurred.

## Bound and Free

Much more could be said regarding the ambiguity of Paragraph 14. What is clear, though, is that it seeks to hold together a tension that is present throughout the *Basis of Union*, but perhaps nowhere else rendered as problematically as it is here. This tension pertains to how the church represents and maintains the apostolic witness while re-imagining and reforming its life for a new time and context. Paragraph 14 reflects a church that sees itself, by necessity, as *bound and free* as it comes to frame its theology of ordained ministry.[22] It is bound to those critical evangelical marks of the church (*notae ecclesia*), Word and Sacrament, that, in D'Arcy Wood's words, "make the church what it is,"[23] and yet free to envisage newly incorporative expressions which centre the whole people of God.

Without question, in its daily practice the UCA has been animated more by freedom than boundedness.[24] Andrew Dutney notes that such a mood was inherent within the antecedent priorities of the Joint Commission on Church Union prior to 1971. He points out that of all the phrases and images of the *Basis*, "pilgrim people, always on the way towards the promised goal"'

---

22  This is indicative of the overall project of organic church union.

23  D'Arcy Wood, *Building on a Solid Basis*, 43. Calvin frames the marks of the true church as where the Word is rightly preached and the sacraments properly administered, John Calvin, *Institutes of the Christian Religion*, Book IV, Paragraph 9, trans. and eds. McNeill and Battles, (Philadelphia, PA: Westminster Press, 1975), 1023.

24  The definition of which is almost always assumed, unarticulated, blurry, and reflective more of a general mood than theological considerations

(BOU, 3), has most caught the UCA's imagination.[25] It also caught what Dutney suggests was the Commission's insistence that "[the UCA] must keep her Church order flexible and free in order to respond to Christ in the new forms of obedience necessary."[26]

Dutney's own reflections, though, presuppose a lot about the nature of that freedom as it corresponds to the continuity of the apostolic faith – to the church's boundedness. The paragraph following the one cited above in *The Church, Its Nature, Function and Ordering*, says:

> This does not mean that the Gospel changes – it is given once-for-all – but it must be related ever afresh to the changing thought patterns of life. Neither do the sacraments change, nor is Christ's provision of ministry for His Church subject to alteration; but the Church must always be seeking to relate her sacramental life to, and give expression to her ministries in, a world where there is often rapid movement in the social groupings which fashion human awareness and provide the forms of human need.[27]

Here, then, the church's freedom is contextualised. It is, indeed, defined by those practices, marks, and beliefs that have come to represent orthodoxy, what Dutney calls, "the essential things" of the faith, which, "the Basis would have us receive and acknowledge ... in a way that keeps us open to the coming of the living Christ."[28] "Receive and acknowledge" bear a lot of weight in this sentence, holding the boundedness dimension.

---

25  Andrew Dutney, "Flexible and Free: An Ecclesiology of Change," *Uniting Church Studies*. 21, no. 1 (June 2017): 9. As if to underline this point, in his opening prayer for the anniversary conference from which this volume of papers has derived, Sean Winter utilised the "pilgrim people" trope.

26  Andrew Dutney, "Flexible and Free," 11. It is supremely ironic, then, that, as Dutney points out, Paragraph 15 of the *Basis* which describes government in the UCA, its councils and oversight structure, "is the only paragraph that does not explicitly anticipate change or even flexibility" (16).

27  CNFO, 86.

28  Andrew Dutney, "Flexible and Free," 15.

Dutney, however, is clearly assuming what the *Basis of Union* states explicitly in Paragraphs 3 & 4, that it was precisely the church's being bound to God's revelation in Christ that animated its freedom to, "place ourselves afresh under God's Word and ask the question, 'What is God's will for us now?'"[29] The church's freedom is not unlimited licence.

"Flexibility and freedom" cannot mean, then, as Barbara Brown Taylor rightly cautions, that the church is, "free to imagine anything we like."[30] At the same time, *boundedness* is a more dynamic phenomenon than rote repetition of past formulas. Rather, as the Joint Commission has it, *freedom* is about *how* the church re-appropriates those 'essential things' for a new age and within rapidly changing contexts, without undermining or calling them into question. It is about *improvisation* of a tradition handed down with faithful attentiveness being paid to the contours of its enduring hallmarks.[31]

## The Challenge and Opportunity of Ordination Theology

One of the primary purposes of ordained ministry in the Reformed/ Evangelical tradition is located in the call to keep the church true to its evangelical kerygma – precisely to keep it appropriately bound to the 'essential things' of the faith. The ordained are "guardians of the Gospel" representatively,[32] on behalf of, and for the sake of the whole church. Ordination is thus a critical element of the UCA's Reformed/Evangelical ecclesiology and place within the one, holy, catholic, and apostolic church. Ministers are charged

---

29  CNOF, 72.

30  Barbara Brown Taylor, *The Preaching Life* (Plymouth, UK: Cowley Publications, 1993), 56.

31  The analogy of the jazz musician who must be intimately aware of the chordal patterns and scales of a piece of music in order to improvise a new rendering is apt.

32  David Bosch, *Transforming Mission: Paradigm Shifts in Theology of Mission* (Maryknoll, New York: Orbis Books, 1991), 474.

with characterising the *bound and free* tension for the whole church whereby it is defined and practised appropriately in light of all the intersecting wider dynamics such as tradition, context, and culture.[33] For Graham Hughes, in line with the classical view, the "three-fold task" (of preaching, presiding, and pastoring) represents the "strict limits" of ordained ministry which should be "articulated and adhered to with scrupulous exactitude."[34] But the "three-fold task" is also the principal means by which the ordained "guard the Gospel" for the wider body.

Hughes brings a certain defensiveness to his thinking (he wants to resist clericalism, regulate clergy power, and curb the potential for ordained ministry "swallowing up all ministry"),[35] yet strict adherence to the "three-fold task" can also be seen as providing precisely the platform for an appropriate freedom pertaining to the practice of ordination. Wanting gently to push Hughes' understanding in terms of its public dimension and repercussions, Stephen Burns asks rhetorically, "However understandable it is that ... Graham Hughes might wish to place clarifying 'limits' on ordained ministry's scope, is it not also the case that the central things of Christian worship imply 'wide reach', invite and foster wider horizons?"[36] Burns continues: "And is not the representative role that is the privilege of liturgical presidency meant to be, and yet capable of being, emboldening of Christians in their shared representative, priestly, public service in God's world?"[37]

---

33  Admittedly, what qualifies as "appropriate" in this context is itself a complicated and subjective matter and often the catalyst of conflict – the limits of orthodoxy have always been somewhat blurry.

34  Graham Hughes, "Limping Priests", 6. Hughes calls this "delimitation." Here the distinction between Minister of the Word and Deacon stipulates the alternative focus between the gathered (MoW) and scattered (Deacon) communities.

35  Graham Hughes, "Limping Priests," 6.

36  Stephen Burns, "Limping Priests" 16. Burns' use of the term 'wide reach' derives from Stephen Pickard's book, *Theological Foundations for Collaborative Ministry* (Farnham: Ashgate, 2009), 85-108.

37  Stephen Burns, "Limping Priests," 16.

Burns is surely right to suggest that the three-fold task, animated and derived from the Word, represents a platform laden with creative promise for an expansive, engaged, and empowered witness. So understood, this witness is one in which the ordained offer a particular kind of oversight and direction, but which is a calling and responsibility of the whole church. The freedom of ordained ministry derives its existence and its character, precisely from the nature of its boundedness, and from the substantive content of that to which it is bound: the Gospel of the living Word, Jesus Christ. Here it is indicative of how the *bound and free* tension works at large. In its boundedness to Jesus Christ, the church's freedom is characterised and informed. For what could be more free than the blowing, convicting, inspiring Spirit of the One who, according to the Creed, was raised from death and who "lives and reigns with the Father" and who shall "come again to judge the living and the dead" and whose 'kingdom will have no end"? Boundedness to Christ by grace, through faith, and participation in his ongoing ministry, is the greatest freedom on earth, and that which disciplines all ministry and all of the church's life.[38] This is the truth that theologically regulates the ordained ministry while also providing the freedom of the pastoral vocation.

My contention here is that it is something along these lines that Paragraph 14 is reaching for but struggles adequately to capture, thus creating confusions that have plagued the UCA's discourse around ordination ever since. It wants to affirm the classical understanding of the Reformed/Evangelical tradition and the purpose, dignity, and place of ordination therein, while also indicating the vast scope, the "wide reach," implied in terms of practice, the wider church's life, and participation of the whole people of God in the ongoing ministry of Christ. For the ordained, preaching, presiding, and pastoring are the historically recognised instruments by which the church is to be encouraged

---

38 That is, it *cannot* be boundedness to anything/one else, not reason, or experience, or tradition, or institutional directives.

and equipped, with a view to maintaining the apostolic witness. These venerable practices of the church relate specifically to the particular trust that has always been associated with the ordained ministry. Being of the Word, the animating agency lies beyond the minister or the church in the eternal will and purposes of the loquacious God (*Deus dixit*), but its character takes on the breadth of prophetic, priestly, pastoral dimensions embodied by Christ, facilitating the freedom of ordination.

## Conclusion

It is worth noting that for all the UCA's circuitous journeys with ordination, all its debates and conversations, in its most recent formal statements,[39] the theology continues to flow readily with the grain of the Reformed/Evangelical tradition and would be immediately recognisable to the framers of the *Basis of Union*. This confirms D'Arcy Wood's conviction that, "The calling, training, setting apart and assigned responsibilities of [ordained] ministers has varied a good deal through history, but the main focus of their role in the church has remained remarkably stable."[40] A recognition and acknowledgment of such stability and the good reasons for it, might help the UCA reengage a dialogue between our ordered ministry and our context.

---

39  Such as the 2008, Basic Affirmations on Ordination, and the more recent Assembly DocByte, "Ordination," available at "DocBytes," Uniting Church in Australia Assembly, accessed April 24, 2023, https://www.assembly.uca. org.au/doctrine/item/856-docbytes#:~:text=DocBytes%20are%20short %20discussion%20starters,point%20to%20further%20reading%20options.
40  D'Arcy Wood, *Building on a Solid Basis: A Guide to the Basis of Union*, 44.

# 6

# The *Basis of Union* and the "Uniting" in the Uniting Church in Australia

John Evans

## Introduction

The Uniting Church in Australia has long since settled into being a denomination within the Australian ecclesial landscape. The *Basis of Union*, however, envisaged a different future for this emerging "new church" beyond denominationalism; beyond being a new church set apart from other churches because of its doctrine and polity. Shortly stated, this new church would be a *uniting* church "within the fellowship of the whole Church Catholic" (BOU, 1). It would, among other things, seek to deepen the faith, and further the mission of the whole church in Australia through fellowship, even union, with other churches. It would have an ecumenical focus through seeking to live and work "within the faith and unity of the One Holy Catholic and Apostolic Church" (BOU, 2). It would not be just a "United" Church of three existing denominations, nor a new denomination within the great sweep of the "Church Catholic". Yes, the Congregational, Methodist and Presbyterian Churches were uniting to achieve that – but once united, this church would go on uniting with other churches because this was "Christ's gift and will for the Church" (BOU, 1).

This paper will examine how the *Basis of Union*, together with the antecedent reports of the Joint Commission on Church Union,[1] set out this vision for this "new church" and how it would operate within the Church Catholic in Australia and in the region of Asia and the Pacific. The paper will remind the numerically

---

1 See FPTC and CNFO.

declining and increasingly denominationally focused church of this original "uniting vision" of the *Basis* and suggests that perhaps the very name "uniting" could be refreshed on the occasion of the jubilee of the *Basis of Union* itself.[2] And finally drawing from the *Basis of Union* itself, the paper offers possible ways the Church may again be engaged in its original ecumenical vision.

## The *Basis of Union* and the Uniting Church's Relations with other Churches

The Uniting Church's life and witness are to be carried out within the faith and unity of the universal church, the Church Catholic, as the *Basis* says.[3] The *Basis of Union* makes clear that a new church, a new denomination, was not created on the document's adoption by the uniting churches. Rather there would be a union of three existing churches who were each already within the One Holy Catholic and Apostolic Church. The foundational document for the Uniting Church was not a Confession of Faith per se, nor even a constitution for this new church, but what its name says, a basis of union.

The very first sentences of this *Basis* sets out this reality for the new Church.

> The Congregational Union of Australia, the Methodist Church of Australasia and the Presbyterian Church of Australia, in fellowship with the whole Church Catholic, and seeking to bear witness to that unity which is both

---

2 The Australian Bureau of Statistics 2011 census indicates 5% of the population is Uniting Church. In the 2016 census this was 3.7%. The figures for the 2021 census indicate the figure has fallen to 2.6%. See "2016 Census Religion," Australian Bureau of Statistics, 27 June 2017, https://www.abs.gov.au/AUSSTATS/abs@.nsf/mediareleasesbyReleaseDate/7E65A144540551D7CA2581 48000E2B85) and Philip Hughes, "Religion in the Census 2021," Christian Research Association, 30 June 2021, https://cra.org.au/religion-in-the-census -2021/

3 See BOU, 1.

Christ's gift and his will for the Church, hereby enter into
union under the name of the Uniting Church in Australia.
They pray this act may be to the glory of God the Father,
the Son and the Holy Spirit. (BOU, 1)

These scene setting sentences from the outset point to an open,
ecumenical and uniting vision for this new church. The following
interpretation of Paragraph 1 will, therefore, focus on the key ideas
of fellowship, ecumenical relations, and the nature of union.

*Fellowship*

The three uniting churches, the Congregational, Methodist and
Presbyterian Churches, prior to the Church's inauguration were
"*in fellowship* with the whole Church Catholic." There is a seamless
continuity with the rich heritage of the whole Church Catholic
and the new church. Indeed "fellowship", *koinonia*, is the word or
concept that is used to characterise such a relationship the Uniting
Church would have with other churches across the "whole Church
Catholic." Fellowship, or *koinonia*, is not just what the Uniting
Church will itself be. As Paragraph 3 states: the Church is the
fellowship of the Holy Spirit, a fellowship of reconciliation. The
Uniting Church will be *in fellowship* with other churches too!

*Ecumenical relations*

And so, when there is the union of these three churches, "the
Uniting Church [itself then] lives and works within the faith and
unity of the One Holy Catholic and Apostolic Church" (BOU, 2).
The starting point in any specific relationship the Uniting Church
may have with other churches is the understanding that they all
stand within this wider fellowship of the Church Catholic.

This is a critical observation. Other churches will have different
starting points for their ecumenical relations. For example, consider
the Lutheran Church of Australia (LCA), with whom the Uniting
Church is currently in formal dialogue. Its Document of Union
for the various strands of Lutheranism in Australia, makes this

85

affirmation: "We believe that true Christians are found in every denomination in which to a greater or lesser degree the marks of the one, holy, Christian Church are present, in spite of existing errors, and we rejoice in the unity of the Spirit that binds all true believers to their one Lord."[4] In other words, while the LCA would consider itself part of the Church Catholic, it would show reserve towards others. Indeed, the Theses of Agreement themselves show how important doctrinal purity is:

> 4.a. We believe that where differences in teaching and practices exist or arise between Churches uniting, these differences are to be removed by willingly submitting to the authority of the Word of God. Where a difference in teaching or practices is a departure from the doctrine of the Bible, such difference cannot be tolerated, but must be pointed out as error, on the basis of clear passages of Holy Writ; and if the error is persisted in, in spite of instruction, warning and earnest witness, it must lead to separation.[5]

An example of this reserve is the attitude of the LCA towards other Lutheran churches. Thus, the LCA only holds associate, not full, membership in the Lutheran World Federation (1993, revised 2001), noting: "Acceptance and entry of the Lutheran Church of Australia into membership of the Lutheran World Federation must not be understood to imply reciprocal church fellowship

---

4 "Theses of Agreement adopted by the United Evangelical Lutheran Church in Australia and the Evangelical Lutheran Church of Australia, Document of Union, 1950, Paragraph 5," Lutheran Church of Australia Commission Theology and Inter-Church Relations, accessed February 11, 2022, https://www.lca.org.au/departments/commissions/cticr/

5 "Theses of Agreement," Doctrinal Statements and Theological Opinions Volume 1, Lutheran Church of Australia Commission Theology and Inter-Church Relations, accessed February 11, 2022, https://www.lca.org.au/departments/commissions/cticr/ . This was adopted in this form on August 12, 1948.

on the part of the Lutheran Church of Australia with any of the member churches."[6]

In contrast, for the Uniting Church, purity in preaching and right doctrine and administration of the sacraments are not the main drivers for the Uniting Church's fellowship with others; rather the other is within the broad stream of the Church Catholic and that to have this relationship is Christ's gift and will.

## The Nature of Union

Although, in a sense, a new church *was* created. Theologically what was actually created was a union of three strands of the ongoing Church Catholic. Indeed, the key focus of this opening clause, and of its Constitution, is the name of this union: "The Uniting Church in Australia."[7] This name itself is a manifestation of Christ's prayer for unity within his church, and not just a name – Uniting – which is a bit different, surprising even, for this new denomination. Importantly this new church, this union, is also itself in fellowship with the whole Church Catholic, and as the *Basis* says a few sentences later, this union must itself "seek a wider unity in the power of the Holy Spirit" (BOU, 1).

There is a reason for this summons to a wider unity. This opening sentence, as has been already noted, affirms that unity – this act of uniting – is "both Christ's gift and his will for the Church." Just as significantly, however, this unity is to be "to the

---

6  It however, could be argued this approach is changing. See Church Fellowship and the LCA (2003) Doctrinal Statements and Theological Opinions Volume 3 D 2. It explains: "A well-defined range of factors has moved the LCA in recent times to modify its ways of relating to other denominations in Australia: the unfolding recognition of common ground with certain other denominations as a result of dialogue and ecumenical relationships; the recognition that members of the LCA can take their place in the Australian interchurch scene without damage to their confessional integrity; and the need for a cooperative approach to ministry in areas of declining membership."

7  See Constitution Clause 1 in "Constitution: Basis of Union, Constitution and Regulations 2018," (Sydney: Uniting Church in Australia Assembly, 2018), 43.

glory of God the Father, the Son and the Holy Spirit" (BOU, 1). This particular union, and I would suggest any subsequent union or future relationship the Uniting Church has with other churches, has a doxological basis. The act of uniting is a way in which this new church glorifies God, the Father, Son and Holy Spirit.

The three uniting churches sought a particular sort of fellowship, indeed an organic union, for themselves. There was indeed a detailed basis, the *Basis of Union*, as to how that union would be established. Significantly, it would be "in sole loyalty to Christ, the living Head of the Church" (BOU, 1). Then in a few short, succinct paragraphs the whole basis of this loyalty to Christ, is unpacked, dealing with this union's understanding of the church, ministry, sacraments, the biblical witness, the creeds, the Reformation and subsequent witnesses, and in an overly-long paragraph, how this union would be governed.

Organic union, was certainly at the forefront of the Uniting Church's thinking. For example, in the Constitution of the Uniting Church, Clauses 38(b)(xii) and (xiii) on the power of the Assembly, presuppose that organic union with other churches will be pursued, and that this will be a central charism of this new church. In the words of these clauses, the Assembly of the Uniting Church has the specific power to:

> (xii) Receive into union any other denomination or any congregation or activity of any other church which in each case adheres to the *Basis of Union*; and
> (xiii) Negotiate and to unite with any other denomination of the Christian Church.

However, further unions were not the only option. Other acts, or signs of unity, were also good in themselves insofar as they may deepen faith or serve the mission of the Church Catholic. So, Paragraph 2 of the *Basis* states:

> The Uniting Church recognises that it is related to other Churches in ways which gives expression, however

88

partially, to that unity in faith and mission. Recalling the Ecumenical Councils of the early centuries, the Uniting Church looks forward to a time when the faith will be further elucidated, and the Church's unity expressed in similar Councils (BOU, 2).

In other words, the Uniting Church thus must seek "ways which give expression" to unity in faith and mission of the whole church, and not just for itself. Perhaps it was a forlorn hope of the *Basis* to anticipate Ecumenical Councils like those that took place in the "early centuries"; but all the same, ways which give expression to the unity of our faith and mission should still be pursued. Neither organic union nor an Ecumenical Council has happened. Nevertheless, as the above quote from Paragraph 2 of the *Basis*, and even those above-quoted clauses of the Constitution acknowledge, other relationships should be pursued. Indeed, towards the end of paragraph 2, two important examples are given:

> The Uniting Church believes that Christians in Australia are called to bear witness to a unity of faith and life in Christ which transcends cultural and economic, national and racial boundaries, and to this end the Uniting Church commits itself to seek special relationships with Churches in Asia and the Pacific. The Uniting Church declares its desire to enter more deeply into the faith and mission of the Church in Australia, by working together and seeking union with other Churches (BOU, 2).

The Uniting Church was thus to seek "special relationships" with the churches of Asia and the Pacific. In the 1950s and 1960s (the time of the work of the Joint Commission on Church Union), Asia and the Pacific were areas where the three uniting churches were actively engaged in missionary activities; more specifically, sending missionaries to these regions. This statement was a reminder to the new church to shift from those colonial relationships and towards seeking insight from those churches themselves. This was a practical outworking of the fellowship the Uniting Church would seek. That may or may not have happened as envisaged. But surprisingly what did happen was that when people from Asia and the Pacific migrated to Australia from these contexts of previous missionary endeavour, these migrants sought a relationship with the Uniting Church.

Some became a part of existing Uniting Church congregations, others formed their own migrant ethnic congregations within the "oversight" of the Uniting Church. Issues inevitably arose as to how the Uniting Church would provide ministry appropriately and in language for these congregations, while at the same time deal with the desire of these congregations to relate back with their home churches. As a result, the "special relationships with churches of Asia and the Pacific" became enshrined in many partnership agreements with these same churches. Moreover, this new multi-cultural reality of the Uniting Church and the new relationships it was embracing, changed the character of the church itself, leading it to declare, in 1985, at the Fourth Assembly, that "We are a multicultural church."[8]

## The *Basis of Union* and the Various Possibilities of Fellowship

The *Basis of Union* makes clear it should be a part of the very being of the Uniting Church to live, perhaps even dance and play, within the great stream of the One Holy Catholic and Apostolic Church. In particular, such engagement is Christ's gift and will; and that seeking such a relationship would be to the glory of God. Moreover, any such work would deepen the faith of the whole Church Catholic, and further the overall mission of God in an increasingly secular Australia – and not for just for the Uniting Church itself and any of its ecumenical partners.

What could then be the nature of this fellowship with other churches in the absence of organic union? Again, the *Basis of Union* usefully provides some guidance as to how the Uniting Church may do this? Three examples are suggested.

---

8 See WEEAMC.

## *To enter more deeply into the Faith (BOU, 2)*

Any analysis as to what the respective churches believe, for example with regard to the Eucharist, would not only relevant to establish the *bona fides*, the good faith, of the parties in relating with one another, but this enquiry would highlight areas where the respective churches may learn from the other in doctrinal understanding, liturgy and practice. An agreement or concordat could thus specify particular areas where there is need for further consideration by the two dialogue partners, individually or together. This, for example, could lead to a shared liturgy or an acceptable alternative form of liturgy, for each church. Where there are points of difference, these should be acknowledged as well, and they may sit as a challenge for either of the two churches, as they consider their life and witness. Furthermore, matters of the faith discerned in such a dialogue may be a relevant consideration more widely within the Church Catholic itself. This perhaps is not "the Ecumenical Councils of the early centuries" which was optimistically referred to in Paragraph 2; but an "Australian take" on say baptism, the eucharist or ministry. This could be an outcome of "entering more fully into the Faith."

## *To enter more deeply into the mission of the Church in Australia (BOU, 2)*

Here the practical outcomes of an agreed relationship, could be many and varied. For example, the Uniting Church has agreements with regard to establishing co-operating parishes, or to provide ministry in rural and isolated areas. It could also have shared community service and educational activities – such as has had been the case with regard to theological education. Such an outcome may specify these particular areas of mission, alternatively, the two churches could agree to a framework for such shared mission endeavours.

To illustrate this possibility, one special area of mission for the Lutheran and Uniting Churches could relate to the faith and witness of the First Peoples of Australia. As noted above, the *Basis of Union* stated that a particular challenge for the union of the three churches was its relationship with the churches of Asia and the Pacific. There was, by implication, much for this new church to learn from these churches of our region, and not simply send them missionaries. Sadly, however, there was no reference in the *Basis of Union* as to what this new church might learn from, let alone how it would relate with, the First Peoples of Australia. In this example, both the Lutheran and Uniting Churches share a common heritage of a deep relationship with the First Peoples of Australia. This could be relevant, perhaps even central, to entering "more deeply into the mission of the Church in Australia".

*To formulate the Church's law to better serve the gospel (BOU, 17)*

The *Basis of Union* sits lightly with regard to the structure and the law of the new church. Indeed, at the time of union only an "Interim Constitution" was adopted.[9] The assumption was its law would evolve: "The Uniting Church acknowledges that the demand of the Gospel, the response of the Church to Gospel, and the discipline which it requires are partly expressed in the formulation of its law" (BOU, 17).

Indeed this evolving nature of its law is well illustrated with the adoption of a new Preamble to the Church's constitution at the Twelfth Assembly in 2009. The original Preamble outlined the background to the *Basis of Union* and then the process as to how the new Church came to be formed at the first Assembly of the Uniting Church in Australia meeting at Sydney on the 22nd of June 1977. The new Preamble repeated much of this, though it significantly now also affirmed that "the Church believes God guided it into union so it believes that God is calling it

---

9 The word "Interim" dropped out of usage after the 12th Assembly, 2009 when the Revised Preamble (see below) was adopted. See note to the Preamble in "Constitution: Basis of Union, Constitution and Regulations 2018," (Sydney: Uniting Church in Australia Assembly, 2018), 42 and the wording of the original Preamble.

to continually seek a renewal of its life as a community of First Peoples and of Second Peoples from many lands". It then outlines the understanding of First Peoples relationship with the "Creator God", the revelation of Jesus Christ, and in turn their experience with the uniting churches.[10] These affirmations and references to the covenantal relationship the Uniting Aboriginal and Islander Christian Congress now shares with the Church begin to fill a gap in the *Basis of Union* and its own Church law. Church law has evolved.

Another illustration of Church law evolving could be the Uniting Church entering into a "concordat" with another church. This could provide a framework for an ongoing relationship between the two churches – beyond say, just the process of dialogue and even shared mission work. Such a framework could specifically express the contemporary "demand of the Gospel."

[It is worth noting that the idea of a concordat was proposed in the 1963 report of the Joint Commission on Church Union. The proposal was for a concordat between the proposed Uniting Church and the already united Church of South India. It lapsed largely because of the opposition to its proposal to include bishops in the Uniting Church as a sign of the unity with the episcopal Church of South India. Still, a concordat was envisaged: but it was not for the Uniting Church to enter into organic union with the Church of South India, but for the purpose of achieving a, widening "unity-in-mission".[11] In this instance such unity would be with regard to how ministry within the respective churches be undertaken.]

◇◇◇

---

10  See RevPreamble.

11  "Through this Concordat, we hope, the Uniting Church will be responding to a God-given sign, and will find itself on the pilgrim road to widening unity-in-mission" (CNFO, 140).

As the *Basis of Union* begins with its uniting vision for the new church, it also ends with that hope: "The Uniting Church prays that through the gift of the Spirit, God . . . will bring it into deeper unity with other Churches" (BOU, 18). As these three examples suggest, organic union may not be envisaged at this time, however, a focus on "deeper unity with other Churches" remains a core feature of the Uniting Church in Australia.

## Uniting Today

The work of the Joint Commission on Church Union and the 1971 *Basis of Union* heralded a new ecumenical vision: a time of uniting, not just for the three denominations, but with others within the Church Catholic. With hindsight we can today see this vision for the new Uniting Church in Australia was perhaps not the beginning, or even a significant station on the way for Christian unity, but the high point for such a vision. The mechanics and practicality of uniting the three churches just drained too much energy from such a broad vision, and the focus became forming the new denomination itself. Moreover, the Australian context for this new church changed enormously in the intervening years since union. This ecumenical dimension of the *Basis of Union* was, however, once important, indeed central for the Uniting Church. It should not be lost. Indeed, I suggest that it is more important than ever as the Uniting Church endeavours to be faithful to Christ the living Head of the Church (BOU, 1) and enter more deeply into the faith and mission of the Church in Australia (BOU, 2).

# 7

# On Not Losing the Way: The Holy Spirit in the *Basis of Union*

Ennis Macleod

## Introduction

An examination of the references to the Holy Spirit in the *Basis of Union* indicates that, contrary to popular belief, there is a pneumatology embedded in the UCA from its beginning. Certainly much more is said of Jesus Christ, but there is much of the Spirit in the *Basis of Union* that can inform the present and future of the UCA. Fifty years ago, the *Basis* was an expression of the ecumenical movement of God's Spirit, and the crafters of the *Basis* saw the need for the Church to have "the gift of the spirit in order that it may not lose the way" (BOU, 3). So, while there is a discernible pneumatology in the *Basis of Union*, the church must be intentional about rebalancing pneumatology and Christology in recognising the Trinitarian relationship between the Son and the Spirit. Therefore, this paper, in dialogue with the strengths and weaknesses of the pneumatology of the *Basis*, is an invitation to discern present and future movements of the Spirit of God to inform the church's journey along the way.

In what follows, I will demonstrate that the *Basis* most often speaks of the Holy Spirit in terms of Gift, gifts, power and unity. The Holy Spirit is the Gift given to the church that unites and empowers those in the church through gifts of leadership and service to do the work of Christ. The language around the person of the Spirit is as *Gift*; source of power and unity, and around the work of the Spirit as the *giver* of gifts and power. I will examine issues around guidance and the Gift of the Spirit, and leadership and the gifts of the Spirit, as well as the connections between unity and the power of the Holy Spirit. I will then explore the implications of these findings.

## What *does* the *Basis* say about the Holy Spirit?

In order to focus on these four elements, I will first note the details of the location and frequency of the references to the Spirit in the *Basis*. Of the 22 references (itemised in the table below), I will discuss 5 of them. I will begin with the Spirit as Gift who guides the church in paragraphs 3 and 18.[1] I could have chosen other purposes of the Gift of the Spirit, but the guidance of the Holy Spirit has much to say to the Church as we continue into the future. Secondly, paragraphs 13 to 16 explain the relationship between gifts and leadership within the Church. However, the Spirit is acknowledged as the giver of these gifts in paragraphs 13 and 14 only. I will focus on the sentence from paragraph 13 where the Church "acknowledges with thanksgiving that the one Spirit has endowed members of Christ's Church with a diversity of gifts," the only sentence in the Basis where the Spirit is the subject of a clause.[2] Finally, I will examine the connection between the power of the Spirit and the unity of the church using the two paragraphs on the sacraments: paragraphs 7 and 8.

---

1 Gift (singular) is always connected with the Holy Spirit in the *Basis*, except where the singular denotes one type of gift given either by Christ (BOU, 1), or the Spirit (BOU, 13 and 14d).

2 In other sections 'gifts' are referenced, but the Spirit's agency is diminished/absent.

Table 1 Mentions of the Holy Spirit in the *Basis of Union*

| Phrase | In paragraphs | N = |
|---|---|---|
| Power of the Holy Spirit | 1, 4, 7, *8*, 10, 16, 17 | 7 |
| Gift of the Holy Spirit | 3, 6, *8*, 10, 18 | 5 |
| Holy Spirit endows with gifts | 13 (Holy Spirit sbj), 14b & 14d | 3 |
| Fellowship of the Holy Spirit | 3, 15, | 2 |
| Father, Son and Holy Spirit | 1, 12 | 2 |
| God gives/sends Holy Spirit | 3 twice (Holy Spirit obj) | 2 |
| Guidance of the Holy Spirit | 14 | 1 |
| Christ poured out the Holy Spirit | 7 (Holy Spirit obj) | 1 |
| Holy Spirit will continue to call | 14c (Holy Spirit sbj) | 1 |
| | **Sub-Total** | 24 |
| | 2 double-ups (in italics) ∴ **Total** | 22 |
| sbj. and obj. denote that "Holy Spirit" is grammatically the subject and object in that mention | | |

## The Spirit as Gift that guides the church

The first characteristic of pneumatology in the *Basis* I will examine is the Holy Spirit as Gift of God. In the Trinity, the Holy Spirit has the nature of Gift, and one expression of that nature in the economy of salvation is the Holy Spirit being given to the church. The church has the Gift of the Spirit, and the Father and the Son are involved with the giving of that Gift. I will examine this idea as it relates to the Holy Spirit as guide to the Church.

In paragraph 3, the giving of the Spirit is referenced twice: "to all people in the Church," and to the Church as guide. In the first instance, the Spirit is actively given, while in the second, the church has "the gift of the Spirit." The Spirit confirms and gives a foretaste of the end to individuals; and the Spirit is with the Church to ensure its actions lead it on the way to "the promised goal." There is clearly a causal connection between the Spirit being given to *individuals* and the *Church* having the Spirit. Thus, the guidance of the Church by the Spirit is dependent on individuals receiving the gift of the Spirit. The church can recognise "the way" because the people of God have a foretaste of the goal against which they can compare the steps being taken.

There is a necessary caveat here. The people of God are *given* the gift of the Holy Spirit, enabling the whole church to *have* the fellowship of the Holy Spirit. Individuals can recognise the 'taste' of the gift of the Spirit, but it is the whole church that discerns the way when it is alert to what the Holy Spirit is saying. This is a vital point. Recognising and valuing the movement of the Spirit entails knowing the Spirit; it requires the church to listen to the diverse voices of the people in the Church. The Spirit who is divine Gift is also the Spirit who is Guide and Paraclete. This is confirmed in paragraph 18, where the church prays that the Gift of God, which is the Holy Spirit, will enable the church to identify and correct any errors that arise during the journey into the future.

### The Spirit as giver of gifts

While the *Basis* recognises the Holy Spirit as Gift and Giver of gifts, it is rather coy about the nature of the gifts of the Spirit, reserving them for equipping members for service and leadership in the Church.[3] In any examination of the gifts of the Spirit, one's first recourse is to Paul's lists of gifts. In Romans 12:6-8, he speaks of the gifts of the Spirit as prophecy, service, teaching, encouraging, giving, leading and showing mercy. In 1 Corinthians 12:8-10; 28-29, he includes the gifts of apostleship and evangelism, discernment, understanding, knowledge, miracle-working, healing, and speaking and interpreting tongues. In addition, any understanding of the gifts of the Spirit should make reference to Isaiah 11:2-3, where the gifts that come with the Spirit are wisdom, understanding, counsel, might, knowledge, and the fear of God. While the *Basis* does acknowledge the Spirit as the one who gives gifts of leadership to those called into ministry, both lay and ordained, the Holy Spirit is not mentioned in relation to the activities of other leaders in the church: "of evangelist, of scholar, of prophet and of martyr," which summon the church to confess the Lord "in fresh words

---

3 Paragraph 13 is the most fulsome paragraph on this subject: "the one Spirit has endowed the members of his Church with a diversity of gifts." The threefold purpose of the church: worshipping, witnessing and service, all are called to service; deaconesses are called to service and witness; worship, described in terms of preaching and sacraments, and witnessing merits no mention in terms of the gifts of the Holy Spirit.

and deeds."[4] The *Basis* omits a vital function of the inspiration of the Holy Spirit: to bring forth fresh expressions of faith and new ways of understanding and communicating the good news of Jesus Christ to emerging generations.

A second understanding of what is given to humanity through the Spirit is in terms of the communication of the grace of God expressed in creation, justification and sanctification. The Christological emphasis of the *Basis* falls heavily on the second of these, justification through Christ: the Spirit of Christ calls people into the church. Nevertheless, the *Basis* shies away from the gifts of the Spirit present in creation, our connection to the earth, the presence of the Spirit since time immemorial, and from the personal gifts of the Spirit that enable sanctification. Additionally, it is absolutely silent on the fruit that involve the emotions of the individual.[5] This reticence in acknowledging the function of the gifts of the Spirit in the affective lives of individuals is a short-coming that has consequences for the present and future of the Church. In this day and age, it is important to acknowledge what Simeon Zahl calls the "affective salience of doctrine;" the connection between doctrinal claims, and the emotions and experiences of people of faith.[6] The gifts of the Spirit and the expression of the Spirit in the lives of God's people have affective dimensions. In the *Basis*, the only expression of the gifts of the Holy Spirit being given to individual men and women is for ministry and service by those in the church.

*The power of the One Spirit*

In the *Basis*, the Holy Spirit and power is quantitatively the most common connection made.[7] The Spirit gives the church power

---

4 See BOU, 11.

5 The words rejoice, love and joy are related to church members in BOU, 1, 7, 8, 14 and 15, but they do not relate to the emotional life of the individual.

6 Simeon Zahl, *The Holy Spirit and Christian Experience* (Oxford: Oxford University Press, 2020), 3-4.

7 BOU, 1, 4, 7, 8, 10, 16, and 17.

in order to, firstly, accomplish the ritual, pastoral, service and ecumenical activities of the church; and secondly, to learn from the Scriptures and to preach from them. In addition, through the power of the Spirit, God acts throughout history in the world, and effects change in people's lives.[8] When we examine the Biblical function of the power of the Holy Spirit we notice a difference. In the OT the Spirit of God is said to come or fall upon prophets or leaders who then "function charismatically and proclaim powerfully both God's judgment and salvation."[9] This idea of the Spirit empowering those gifted to proclaim or act according to God's purposes can be traced in the New Testament, particularly in Luke and Acts, provoking prophecy around the births of John and Jesus, and in Jesus' ministry, and in Paul's writings.[10] After Christ's ascension, the power of the Holy Spirit is associated with evangelism through "signs and wonders" to those outside the group who are brought in, and then as bringing strength and hope to the believers. This linking of the power of the Spirit with individuals charismatically is absent in the *Basis*.

## The Spirit of Unity, Union, Uniting

Unity is spoken of in the first paragraph of the *Basis* as "Christ's gift and will for the Church," while seeking "wider unity" is in the power of the Holy Spirit. In the *Basis* we are united in Christ, but it is in the power of the Holy Spirit that unity is achieved or sought, and that we "grow together into Christ." Indeed, it has been part of the doctrine of the Church since before the first Creeds that the Spirit and the one, holy, catholic, and apostolic Church are connected; that "because there is only one Spirit of Christ ... there is

---

8  These activities are demonstrated in the Christological statement in paragraph 4, "...in the power of the Holy Spirit...in his own strange way, Christ constitutes, rules and renews [those called] as his Church."

9  Castelo, *Pneumatology: A Guide for the Perplexed* (London: Bloomsbury, 2015), 31.

10  Castelo, *Pneumatology*, 36-40.

only one body, which is the Body of Christ."[11] Most often, "unity" being achieved in the "power of the Spirit" is in reference to the wider, universal, catholic Church, except in paragraphs 7 and 8 on the sacraments peculiar to that one Church.

The Holy Spirit is active in the sacrament of Holy Communion, such that it is their own faith, and the gift and power of the Spirit that enables the people of God to commune with Christ, and to "grow together into Christ." The power of the Holy Spirit enables the people of God to be one with Christ. In paragraph 7, those who receive baptism into Christ's body are to be united, "in the power of the one Spirit." In both sacraments unity enables the church to continue the work of Christ in the world. But, most importantly, a close reading of paragraph 7 reveals that an attribute of the Holy Spirit is unity; there is "the one Spirit," and the power of this oneness enables the church, those baptised into Christ, to be united. The overarching purpose of the *Basis*, to express the faith that unites the Church, is therefore demonstrated to be at heart a work of the Holy Spirit, and expresses the character of the Holy Spirit.

## Implications

### Pneumatology and Christology

While the *Basis* acknowledges the gifts and activity of the Spirit in leading and guiding the church, when it comes to governing the Church, the *Basis* states that "Christ alone is supreme in his Church and ... he may speak to it though any of its councils" (BOU, 15). This focus on Christ's supremacy ignores the activity of the Holy Spirit in decision-making. In addition, a preoccupation with the acts of the Holy Spirit's being understood only in terms of acting on behalf of Christ focuses attention on an intellectual

---

11 Yves Congar, *I Believe in the Holy Spirit: The Complete Three-Volume Work in One Volume*, trans. David Smith (Crossroad: New York, 2019), 2:15.

understanding of faith. In the *Basis*, activities ascribed to the Holy Spirit are: to make Christ known; to enable the Church to complete the mission given by Christ; to give gifts through Christ to maintain the order of the Church; to make known God's salvation through Christ to the individual; and to enliven the sacraments of baptism and Holy Communion in which the primary instigator and agent is Jesus Christ. For example, while paragraph 4 has Christ calling people "in the power of the Holy Spirit" to discipleship, we can go some way towards understanding and experiencing Christ's "own strange way" if we examine being in Christ and being open to the Holy Spirit with equal emphasis. Certainly, the Holy Spirit is the Spirit of Christ, but, contrary to this paragraph, the church is co-constituted, co-ruled and renewed by both Christ and the Holy Spirit.[12] An underdeveloped pneumatology results in the Holy Spirit having no agency of her own, and the Church being unevenly responsive to the inspiration and guidance of the Holy Spirit. The Spirit becomes, not a Person to be known, but a conduit for the Person of Christ. This preoccupation with the Holy Spirit's alignment with Christ focuses attention on the cerebral experience of faith. It risks ignoring the different ways people experience the leading of the Holy Spirit.

Pneumatology being subsumed into Christology has three consequences: (1) reducing acknowledgment of the gifts of the Spirit to those for leadership and service; (2) devaluing individuals' experiences of the Spirit; and (3) ignoring experiences of the Holy Spirit that are culturally different from one's own. Today, it is vital that we move on from a Christological overemphasis which ignores the agency of the Spirit and thus devalues God's activity in the world. It is necessary to be intentional in acknowledging that the Spirit moves in fresh ways throughout the world; that the

---

12  See Yves Congar's section on the two missions of Christ and the Holy Spirit, and the co-institution of the church. Congar, *I Believe in the Holy Spirit*, 2:7-10.

Spirit's moving can be discerned when an appropriate balance is maintained between Christology and pneumatology.

Nevertheless, even when the Church downplays the activity of the Holy Spirit, the Spirit continues to move. In an examination of the universal Church just in the last hundred years or so, we can identify movements of the Spirit that brought new life to the church. In the early missionary movement (even with its trappings of colonialism) the Spirit is sent into the world to spread God's good news. In the ecumenical movement of the mid-twentieth century we see an expression of unity which is part of the Spirit's character. The charismatic renewal of the traditional churches in the late twentieth century can be seen as an expression of the activity of the Holy Spirit in giving gifts to equip the Church. In liberation theology we can see God's Spirit of justice at work, finding expression in the UCA in the formation of Uniting Aboriginal and Islander Christian Congress and the adoption of the Revised Preamble to the Constitution. None of these movements of the Spirit can be relegated to history. All of them continue to express the activity of the Holy Spirit today, and will go with the church into the future. They all feed in to movements of the Spirit today which acknowledge that diversity is an expression of the Spirit's creativity expressed in the infinite variety of creation, of culture and of the natural world.

*The creative divine Spirit*

In the *Basis*, pneumatology is mostly expressed in terms of the work of the Trinity in the Church. But there is a broader understanding of the immanent Trinity that expresses growing understanding of the Church throughout history and into the future. In the history of the Church, the nature of the Holy Spirit has been variously named. The *Basis*'s pneumatology is certainly in line with Augustine's calling the Holy Spirit love and unity within the immanent Trinity. But, in the ancient hymn, the Holy Spirit is also called *Creator Spiritus*. The Spirit is the one who hovered over the waters at creation, the one who blows where she will. The Holy

Spirit creates diversity; not just in the variety of gifts given to the church, but also in the creativity she inspires in the Church. In the *Basis*, unity is taken to be the primary expression of the power of the Holy Spirit. The Gift of the Spirit enables unity, and the Spirit gives gifts to people in the Church to foster unity, but not at the expense of variety and creativity.

While the Christology of the *Basis* orients the UCA to a Body of Christ ecclesiology, an expansion of the pneumatology of the *Basis* will enable the UCA to continue into the future in the power of the Holy Spirit. The Holy Spirit calls on the Church to accept that different ways of being and doing express the creativity of the Holy Spirit; that glorying in opportunities to experience what it is like to be the outsider, even when there is discomfort, enhances unity. Additionally, we continue into the future aware of our responsibility for the earth created out of the chaos over which the Spirit hovered, and into which God breathed the Spirit. Finally, we continue into a future where there is a dearth of hope. The Spirit moves in response to the need of the world. We have good news of hope to share with the hopeless. I pray we will respond to the call of the Spirit to take the Good News to those who have lost hope in a good future. In order to grasp these responsibilities, the church needs to continue to discern what the Spirit is saying to the church, and pray for the power and guidance of the Holy Spirit promised to the Uniting Church in its foundational document.

# Cross-Cultural Engagements

# 8

# Translating the *Basis of Union*: Learning from Heart Languages

Ji Zhang

## Introduction

"*The Basis of Union* in Heart Languages" is a project of translation of the National Assembly. It builds upon the Church's history of multicultural and cross-cultural ministry and listens to the calling to "seek a wider unity in the power of the Holy Spirit" (BOU, 1).

To mark the 50th anniversary of the *Basis*, I will highlight a theological paradox: unity and mission are mutually inclusive and inform each other. In unity, the Church discovers God's mission in Australia; in mission, the Church embraces diversity as the gifts of the Spirit within the Christ's Body. Based on the experience of our translation project, I present this paper as a theological reflection to engage a dialogue between context and theology.

## We Are a Multicultural Church

"*The Church as the fellowship of the Holy Spirit confesses Jesus as Lord over its own life*" (BOU, 3).

In 1985, the 4th Assembly adopted a statement, "The Uniting Church is a Multicultural Church".[1] Then the Church recognised that successive governments had removed racial criteria from Australian immigration policies. Later the Church acknowledged our multicultural ministry was built upon the missionary history as

---

1  The Uniting Church in Australia, *Minutes of the Fourth Assembly* (Melbourne: Uniting Church Press, 1985), 180-1.

former missionaries developed cross-cultural bridges that enabled migrants to be part of the Uniting Church.[2] In 2015, the Assembly celebrated this 30-year journey, and affirmed that our diversity is a gift of the Spirit to the Church.[3]

Our mission has displayed a multi-directional movement of the Spirit. The Spirit has moved the hearts of migrants, refugees, and students from many lands; they have come to this ancient Land and called Australia home. Today around 45 languages, 15 of which are languages of our First Peoples, are used each week across our congregations. The Body of Christ is not only one, but also many.

The Assembly has translations of the *Basis of Union* in ten languages: Arabic, Chinese (simplified and traditional), Fijian, Indonesian, Kiswahili, Korean, Nuer, Samoan, Spanish (under revision) and Tongan. The Assembly encourages its culturally and linguistically diverse (CALD) communities to read the *Basis* in heart languages to deepen the understanding about the unity and the governance of the Church. Together with the English version, the translations are digitally available in the searchable platform *Illuminate*.[4] Eight translations have been published as large posters for public display and presented in colourful backgrounds.[5] Congregations can download their language(s), print, and display the poster(s) together with the English version. Research towards a plain English version has begun, building upon the First Peoples' bible translation experience.

*"Christians in Australia are called to bear witness to a unity of faith and life in Christ which transcends cultural and economic, national and racial boundaries"* (BOU, 2).

---

2 Multicultural Ministry, *Migrant-Ethnic Congregations in the Uniting Church in Australia* (Sydney: National Assembly, 1999), 2-3.

3 National Assembly, accessed 8 February 2022, https://assembly.uca.org.au/images/UCA-WE-ARE-A-MULTICULTURAL-CHURCH-30TH-ANNIVERSARY-WEB.pdf

4 "Illuminate," Camden Theological Library, https://illuminate.recollect.net.au

5 "Basis of Union Posters Hub (Multiple Languages), Uniting Church in Australia Assembly, https://ucaassembly.recollect.net.au/nodes/view/725

These translations speak for our unity in faith and life in Christ. Indeed, God is bringing the world into the Church through the people of God. The fact that the Church consists of the CALD communities is a witness that the Church is both product and agent of mission. Half a century ago, the CALD people were the recipients of Church's mission to the margins; now they have embodied God's mission in and from the margins.

## A journey of discovery

"*It is related to other Churches in ways which give expressions, however partially, to that unity in faith and mission*" (BOU, 2).

Whoever interprets the *Basis* will also be interpreted by it. Our theological wrestling through translation involves deep transformation and profound discovery.[6] My journey began in 1999 when I was a postgraduate student in Boston. I read the *Basis*, and wrestled with this sentence: "They give praise for God's gifts of grace to each of them in years past; they acknowledge that none of them has responded to God's love with a full obedience…" (BOU, 1). In my reflection, I recognised that there was a calling of God in Australia. Standing before this calling, nothing was so important that could keep three churches apart. Then I returned to Australia and discovered my calling to serve the Uniting Church.

The Chinese translation began in 2013 when the China Christian Council (CCC) invited the Uniting Church in Australia (UCA) to share our experience of "being and becoming a uniting church". After the conference it became obvious that the *Basis* had to be retranslated. The conference challenged old assumptions, and the dialogue produced new insights. Then the hermeneutical circle continued, moving from the context to the text. Now I understand

---

6 "Found in Translation: Sharing the Basis of Union in Heart Languages". National Assembly, accessed 7 February 2022, https://uniting.church/found-in-translation-the-basis-of-union-in-heart-languages/

why the *Basis* had four versions between 1957 and 1971 as the result of dialogues among the three churches.[7]

To maintain the principle of textual fidelity, I studied the negotiations among three denominations. To be contextually meaningful, I worked with two translators from the CCC, Mrs Gu Jinqqin and Rev Zhao Chengyi, using the liturgical languages of the Chinese Church. Over the years, I had some conversations with the Pacific leaders about the nuance of specific expressions, like "mutual submission," discussions with the UCA theologians about Methodist "Leaders," and debates with Chinese ministers about the difference between "Minister" and "Pastor." After the consultation within the Chinese National Conference, the translation was finalised in 2020.

When this current paper was first presented at the 50th anniversary conference, Mrs Gu, secretary of Overseas Department, shared a significant insight. The Church in China revised the 2008 edition of its *Constitution* with an amendment: from "a post-denominational church" to "a uniting church". Gu said: "Unity is an imperative endeavour to take, because it's not merely human work, but also a call of God and a gift of God, as it is also reiterated in your *Basis* that unity is both Christ's gift and will for the church."[8] The Church in China is not yet in a full status of being united; it is in an unceasing process of uniting with Christ. "Therefore, a uniting church was agreed as a better term than a united church to be used to describe the current state of the Church in China."[9] The amendment of the CCC's

7 D'Arcy Wood, "The Basis of Union: its formation 1957-1971", in *A Pilgrim People: 40 Years On* (Victoria: Uniting Church National Historical Society, 2018), 172-79. Also see, Michael Owen, *Back to Basics: studies on the Basis of Union of the Uniting Church in Australia* (Victoria: The Joint Board of Christian Education, 1996), 8-104.

8 Ivy Gu, "The Basis of Union at 50: a dialogue between the CCC and the UCA" (conference presentation), Pilgrim Theological College, Melbourne, 27 November 2021.

9 Gu, "The Basis of Union at 50."

*Constitution* sets a policy direction for: a) theological formation for future ministers; b) continuing education for clergy and the laity; and c) being the Church in and for the world through diakonia.

The translation has led to a profound discovery: Christ and his Church are inseparable. Just as Geoff Thompson puts it, reading the paragraphs 3 and 4 of the *Basis* is deeply disturbing, and it calls for our obedience to the Word of God.[10] In this partnership, I also see the Spirit at work, moving both churches into mutual witness and calling individuals into service. Unity in partnership is not about sameness but rather wholeness in Christ, "bearing with one another in love, making every effort to maintain the unity of the Spirit in the bond of peace" (Eph 4: 2-3). The Spirit also bears witness to the Son and the Father.

## Learning about Grace

*"It remembers the special relationship which obtained between the several uniting Churches and other Churches of similar traditions, and will continue to learn from their witness and be strengthened by their fellowship"* (BOU, 2).

Rev Eseta Meneilly completed the Fijian translation in dialogue with Rev Dr Tevita Banivanua, a past president of the Methodist Church in Fiji.[11] She worked through the problem of "translating the untranslatable." The common Christian term "grace" has no equivalent translation in Fijian. In the Fijian Bible, "grace" is translated as *loloma* which is "love" in English. This problem highlights two issues. First, in Fijian, the word "love" is all-encompassing, like the phrase "God is love" (1 John 4:16). Second,

---

10 Geoff Thompson, *Disturbing Much Disturbing Many: Theology provoked by the Basis of Union* (Northcote: Uniting Academic Press, 2016), 27-32, 42-43.

11 Eseta Meneilly, "The Basis of Union 50: Grace is *loloma soli wale*" (conference presentation), Pilgrim Theological College, Melbourne, 27 November 2021.

the multilayered meaning of "grace" must be demonstrated and set apart from *loloma*.

The dialogue between text and context leads to a further discovery. In Fijian culture "grace" is not only an idea, but also an act. Instead of thinking "what grace is," the interpretation is focused on "what grace does." God's grace emerges out of God's very being – God is love – and overflows into the whole world. In Fijian *"loloma savu"* means "love overflowing" or "love running over."

When this expression is put in the context of "the sovereign grace of God" (BOU, 3), a further interpretation is required to explain "what grace does". The Fijian expression, *"loloma soli wale,"* literally means "love given freely." This expression provides a link between grace and salvation.

This dialogue produces a remarkable insight. God's grace does not only enable the whole work of salvation in Christ, but also "love given freely" guides people into faith by the Spirit. The previous sentence says, "God has sent forward the Spirit that people may trust God as their Father, and acknowledge Jesus as Lord" (BOU, 3). It could be interpreted that "love given freely" is sent forward with the Spirit from God's outpouring love. It could be further inferred that God's grace is the outwardly expressed will of God. Therefore, *"loloma soli wale"* is unconditional.

Rev Meneilly rightly concludes that *"loloma soli wale"* means that no matter what the circumstance is, no matter how ugly the situation is like the pandemic, or how unrighteous human behaviour becomes, there is always God's grace – "love given freely" – reaching out from the depth of God's love.

The Uniting Church has a willingness "to learn from their witness and be strengthened by their fellowship" (BOU, 2), and the commitment in relationship with others is a sign of maturity. In the multicultural society, God's grace is also an action pouring love into the space of differences. Indeed, the Church needs this space for grace to live with many differences represented by languages, cultures, histories, and theologies. God's grace – *loloma soli wale* – will enable cross-cultural ministry by the self-giving love of God.

## One Spirit and diverse gifts

*"God in Christ has given to all people in the Church the Holy Spirit as a pledge and foretaste of that coming reconciliation and renewal which is the end in view for the whole creation"* (BOU3).

The project participants have made this observation: none of the translators were part of the UCA at union; the First People's voice was absent in the *Basis*. Reading the *Basis* in heart languages has led to new discovery that the Spirit is at work through us. It is the Spirit itself "bearing witness with our spirit" (Romans 8:16), so that we are the children of God.[12] Our task is not only translating a document received from the past, but also being drawn into the Spirit's witness for the future.

This vision displays radical openness. This Spirit enlivened all people cannot be boxed in a sociological understanding about multicultural togetherness. We also anticipate the coming reconciliation and renewal of all things. For the CALD leaders, it is the Land of the First Peoples that has first accepted us as migrants, indeed all the Second Peoples, and the Land has allowed our cultures to take root in Australia. The Spirit of God also feeds the Church with the gift of cultures along the way.

On behalf of the Tongan community, Rev Dr Jason Kioa presented the Tongan translation and reflected on the nature of language. English has been a dominating language throughout the missionary history in the Pacific. "There is power in language. In the past, the Tongan communities, together with many Pacific

---

12 I was inspired by John Wesley's sermon when I reflected the nature of the Spirit in the Church. John Wesley, "The Witness of the Spirit: Discourse 1", in *Witness of Faith: historic documents of the Uniting Church in Australia*, ed, Michael Owen (Melbourne: Uniting Church Press, 1984), 193-200.

peoples, left behind our identities in colonialism". "The people must not now lose our languages in the Uniting Church." The reason that the Tongan translation is presented in a two-page poster is because the language is narrative in nature. It belongs to the oral tradition and articulates meaning through stories not concepts. This linguistic identity is at the centre of cultural identity. It cannot be reduced to a one-page English poster. Otherwise, the context journey of the community will be lost.

The Uniting Church needs a theology of diversity to see the Church as the fellowship of the Holy Spirit. The Spirit has been central to the life of the Church since its inception.[13] The Spirit is in the presence of difference guiding the Church in its relations with other faiths.[14]

To unpack the nature of diversity, the CALD leaders reflected a problem that diversity has been externalised from the talk of unity. Some people's imagination of diversity is limited by the western conceptual framework. It is assumed that unity is a numerical oneness, like the number "1," in which there is only sameness. Then many cultures are viewed as differences and become a secondary order to the sameness. This is an ontological divide: the one above and the others are below.[15] Consequently our diversity is treated as a problem to unity. The heart of the problem, however, is the assumption of numerical oneness; difference is excluded from sameness.

13 Christopher Walker, "Discerning the Work of the Holy Spirit", in *Building on the Basis: papers from the Uniting Church Australia Assembly Working Groups on Doctrine and Worship*, ed Christopher Walker (The Assembly of the Uniting Church in Australia, 2012), 13-25.

14 Keith Rowe, "Fellowship in the Presence of Difference: Christian Witness in Multifaith Australia", in *Being and Doing Church: a Uniting Church perspective*, ed, Christopher Walker (The Assembly of the Uniting Church in Australia, 2015), 57-64.

15 Ji Zhang, "A Trinitarian Model of Cross-cultural Ministry," *Uniting Church Studies* Vol 18 (June 2012), 47-58.

Reading the *Basis* in heart languages has led to a new understanding. In Chinese, unity is both noun and verb and it has two meanings: "联合 *lianhe* – uniting for completeness" and "联和 *lianhe* – uniting in harmony". The connotation of both terms embraces different members, just like a family is incomplete without all members, a dynasty cannot be prolonged without harmony among the peoples.

*"It acknowledges with thanksgiving that the one Spirit has endowed the members of Christ's Church with a diversity of gifts, and that there is no gift without its corresponding service"* (BOU, 13).

The *Basis* affirms the diversity as the gifts of the Spirit, just as unity is the gift of Christ.

The quote above also follows the biblical witness that the Church was born in the Pentecost by the Spirit. The Spirit still does two things through mission: a) enabling a diversity of gifts; and b) matching gift with corresponding service. The Church, therefore, will order its life for mission and provide opportunities for men and women to exercise ministry with their gifts of the Spirit.

The Spirit does not divide; it sets all people free. "Where the Spirit of the Lord is, there is freedom" (2 Corinthians 3:17). The Spirit will guide our witness through cultures and languages into the unity of completeness in Christ, so we are also liberated and justified. "For all who are led by the Spirit of God are children of God" (Romans 8:14).

## The Spirit of Creation

*"The Uniting prays that, through the gift of the Spirit, God will constantly correct that which is erroneous in its life, will bring it into deeper unity with other Churches, and will use its worship, witness and service to God's eternal glory through Jesus Christ the Lord. Amen".* (BOU, 18)

In 1985, in the same year of the formation of the Uniting Aboriginal and Islander Christian Congress, the 4th Assembly made an amendment to the theology of the Spirit. "The Uniting Church in Australia adopt for its normal liturgical usage the original form of the Nicene Creed confessing the Holy Spirit "who proceeds from the Father" without adding the phrase "and the Son' (in Latin 'filioque')".[16] The removing of the filioque clause does not imply any change in the Church's adherence to the doctrine of the Trinity, but recognises that the importance to amend our theology and renew ecumenical relation with the Orthodox tradition. This amendment opens a door for exploring the presence of the Spirit in this Land.

The Spirit of the Father is the Spirit of creation.[17] The *Preamble to the Constitution* says: "The First Peoples had already encountered the Creator God before the arrival of the colonisers; the Spirit was already in the land revealing God to the people through law, custom and ceremony."[18] The Spirit lives in the Land. The First Peoples have taught us, the Land also lives in us. The whole creation has been created and sustained by the Triune God that we know in Christ who is the second Person of the Trinity.[19] The Spirit of redemption in Christ and the Spirit of creation are not two spirits; they both proceed from to the Triune God.

It is our shared experience that the translation of the *Basis of Union* is incomplete unless the translation of Preamble is completed. It is because the *Basis* needs to be read together with the Preamble. The naming of the Spirit will move the Church's vision beyond ecclesial unity towards the communion with God. Our unity still remains hidden in God's mission – by the Spirit of

---

16  "Re Nicene Creed", *Assembly Resolution 85.52.1*, the 4th Assembly the Uniting Church in Australia (1985).

17  Jürgen Moltmann, *The Spirit of Life: a universal affirmation* (Minneapolis: Fortress, 1992), 8-10.

18  RevPreamble, paragraph 3.

19  Ji Zhang, "Christology of the Preamble – an antidote to Neoliberalism," *Uniting Church Studies* Vol 22. No.1 (June 2019), 61-70.

redemption in Christ and the Spirit of creation – moving the world towards harmony. This unity of the Church will also include our cultural and linguistic diversities and take root in the Land.

"See, I am making all things new" (Revelation 21:5). In the Kingdom of God, there is a consummation of all things. There, the diversity of God's creation is not swallowed into a divine singularity but transformed into the communion with the Triune God in a Christ-like resurrection. The Spirit of the Father will move our hope beyond the limits of the Church in order to see that the same Spirit is moving the whole creation into the unity of harmony – reflecting God's will in Christ. Then the people of God will sing a universal doxology to praise the Creator in their heart languages.

## Conclusion

Unity and mission are mutually inclusive; they inform each other. The *Basis* captured the movement of the Spirit over half a century ago when the churches answered God's calling towards unity in faith and mission. Celebrating the 50th anniversary of the *Basis*, the translation project discerns the same question: "What is God doing in God's world?" Reading the *Basis* in our heart languages is part of Assembly's intercultural priority, moving from multicultural togetherness to intercultural wholeness. The stories of this paper illustrate the dynamics of unity and mission. Theological reflection has also led to the naming of the Spirit.

Although the Trinity is not explicitly stated in the *Basis*, the dynamics of the trinitarian movement is present. The Church is called into existence by God in this Land to "seek a wider unity in the power of the Holy Spirit" (BOU, 1). The Church is "the fellowship of the Holy Spirit" (BOU, 3) to "witness a unity of faith and life in Christ" (BOU, 2). The congregation is the embodiment of this "fellowship of the Spirit in Christ" (BOU, 15). The Church "belongs to the people of God on the way to the promised end"; and "prays that through the gift of the Spirit, God will constantly

117

correct that which is erroneous in its life, and will bring it into deeper unity with other Churches" (BOU, 18).

The gifts of the Spirit have allowed us to see unity and diversity as a set of trinitarian relationships. Within the life of the Trinity, unity and diversity form a paradox of the inner relationships among the Persons. The unity of the Father, the Son, and the Holy Spirit, and the diversity represented by the three Persons, are not understood as logical opposites, but rather the dynamics of relational wholeness. Within the Trinity, there is God's unity of harmony: the one and the many can either be both affirmed or together rejected.

# 9

# Cultural Identity and the *Basis of Union*: A Non-white Migrant Musing

## Hee Won Chang

No person is the same. No Uniting Church is the same. Just as each of us is uniquely different so are the different parts of the Uniting church. Theologically, culturally, racially, and politically many of our congregations are vastly different. We are deeply divided on some issues but remain under the same roof as the Uniting Church, so then who are we? What holds us together? These are the questions I will explore in this paper. I will do so in the form of a non-white migrant musing.[1]

As a non-white migrant, I am often asked where are you from? And I find myself explaining who I am, trying to resist being pigeonholed and stereotyped while still being me.[2] The Uniting Church is often stereotyped and pigeonholed and at times we have failed to communicate fully who we are as a church. For me, constantly seeking to answer who I am is tiring, but it allows me to develop a language about myself. It allows me to develop my story and tell that story with my own words.

As Christians, of course, we are also part of the story of Christ: the One crucified and risen shapes us, and as we take part we become a story. That story shapes and nurtures us. It gives us identity, a distinctive mark that sets us apart from the world. In

---

1 This is a deliberate term I use for myself because I refuse to be called "coloured" or "culturally and linguistically diverse (CALD)" which mask whiteness as the norm.

2 If I am vocal, I am too western and if I am silent I am the passive oppressed Asian woman. The Uniting Church on the other hand is sometimes seen as too justice oriented or not biblical enough.

the Uniting Church there is a *story* of how we came together. Three denominations came together to birth what is now called the Uniting Church *in* Australia.[3] There is a founding document, the *Basis of Union* that sets our call to be a uniquely Australian church and to live and be a church open to constant reform under Christ. But then, at forty-four years of age with a founding document fifty years old, the church seems to be consumed with conversations around decline, survival and a need for a change. And now with the experience of the Pandemic and the new normal upon us, we are challenged with internal and external issues.[4] As "we look to the future and consider afresh our life together"[5] we are told that "it is obvious we cannot stay the way we are."[6] And we ask again who are we: "as we look to the future, what is God saying to us as the Uniting Church about how we order our life"?[7]

Who are we and where are we headed; we ask ourselves. And at times I wonder if the UCA is going through a mid-life-identity crisis? Has the church lost its calling? Is it time "to hear anew" our call? (BOU, 1). At times like this, when we are still discovering what post-pandemic life will be like, when our future seems masked, when change is upon us and we are dying, how does the *Basis* speak into this moment of our identity crisis? Does it provide a common identity for the church's diverse membership? As we are thrown into the new normal, and urged to move forward, to adapt and to

---

3  The 'in' is important. It is not Uniting Church of Australia. We have left being 'of' a particular church to being a church in this land now called Australia.

4  Recent report by the Assembly Standing Committee, *Act 2: Considering Afresh Our Life Together* highlights some of the challenges faced by the Uniting Church. See https://uniting.church/act2/

5  Colleen Geyer, "Introduction from the General Secretary to *Act 2: Considering Afresh Our Life Together*," Uniting Church in Australia Assembly, accessed April 25, 2023, https://uniting.church/consideringafresh/

6  Geyer, "Introduction."

7  This are the introducing words of the Act 2 project (see https://form.jotform.com/203201030312024)which echo the words of Andrew Dutney in an article written in 2017. Andrew Dutney, "Flexible and Free: An Ecclesiology of Change," *Uniting Church Studies*, Vol.21, No.1 June (2017): 9.

change, how does the *Basis* guide us? What language and image does the *Basis* provide to inform and build on our identity?

And to be clear, this essay is just a non-white migrant musing, I do not claim that this is the identity of the church, nor do I ponder how the *Basis* was put together with what intention. That is not the focus of this essay for there are enough talks on what it was meant to be. Rather this is an invitation for you to read, wrestle and engage with the *Basis* like I have and see where it leads you, see if it leaves you a mark.

## Our purpose and identity: "to serve the world for which Christ died"[8]

The *Basis* was written for a particular time and place, yet it has the ability to invite and "speak into other time and places."[9] It invites me – a non-white migrant woman living through a Pandemic – to read it in this particular context. And our Pandemic and post-Pandemic context is the world turned upside down. Our way of living shattered, and the problems of the world were exposed. It felt like God took the world, turned it upside down and gave it a good shake. The way we live, work and play all came to a stop. The way we gather and do church stopped. The world we know has changed and people comment there is no going back. When the Uniting Church was inaugurated on 22 June 1977, a journey into the unknown began; so yes as a church, there is no going back.

However, when we say there is no going back, what are we saying we are not returning to? Surely, it must mean not going back to the world of inequality, patriarchy, poverty, climate change, racism (and the list goes on) that was so prevalent in the world. What is the UCA committing to leave behind, or to have left behind, and is now committing to bring forth? Have we left at

---

8 BOU, 1.
9 Geoff Thompson, *In His Own Strange Way: A Post-Christendom Sort of Commentary on the Basis of Union* (Unley: MediaCom Education, 2018), 5.

all? As a church how are we to journey in this new world? Will our "future directions" guide us? Will new vision and strategy save us? How is our identity formed in this new normal? How is our identity shaped by the *Basis*?

The *Basis* makes it quite clear *who* we belong to. Our identity comes from the One crucified and risen.[10] Our identity comes from being present to the world, here and now. As a church we are "an instrument through which Christ may work and bear witness to himself" (BOU, 3). We are "built upon the one Lord Jesus Christ. The Church preaches Christ the risen crucified One and confesses him as Lord to the glory of God" (BOU, 3). And it continues: "in love for the world, God gave the Son to take away the world's sin" (BOU, 3). And we are to be "committed to serve the world for which Christ died" (BOU, 1).[11]

In Christ, the church is to be rooted right here and right now. We are to be deeply present to the realities and the struggles in the now. We are not to avoid the present reality and look elsewhere for hope. Rather because we are deeply rooted, here and now, we can be hopeful that one day "the kingdom of this world has become the kingdom of our Lord and of the Christ" (BOU, 1). In other words, let us "deal with our shit" now instead of looking elsewhere. Let us stop giving lip service to the First Peoples and truly engrain the covenant we have made with them. Let us stop merely celebrating being a multicultural church and truly become one. Let us act on climate urgency before blood is on our hands. We are called to form a special relationships with Churches in Asia and the Pacific (see BOU, 2), and as Maratja Dhaamarrandi has said in reference to *Yolŋu*, more broadly also.[12] In the mutuality of such relationships, what, for instance, is our responsibility for our sisters and brothers in the Pacific who are screaming, "We will not drown"?

---

10  For a more detailed discussion see Chapter 2 in Geoff Thompson, *Disturbing Much, Disturbing Many: Theology Provoked by the Basis of Union* (Northcote, Uniting Academic Press, 2016).
11  BOU, 1.
12  "The Basis of Union as *rom*: a Yolŋu perspective", pp. 23-29 this volume.

The *Basis* commits the church to the world Christ so loved and died for. It presses us to be in the present, to be in the now, and to "acknowledge one another in love and joy" (BOU 1). And it makes it clear that Christ is the one who holds us together and who "feeds the church with Word and Sacraments" (BOU, 3). It also reminds us that the church is gifted with the Spirit, that it "may not lose the way" (BOU, 3). As a church we are "able to live and endure through the changes of history only because its Lord comes, address, and deals with people in and through the news of his completed work" (BOU, 4). We are able to live with difference and endure hard conversations only because of Christ who comes, addresses and deals.

## Our location: Living "in-between...towards a promised goal"

As we commit ourselves to serve the world, the *Basis* expresses some specific images on what that might look like; the church as being the pilgrim people of God,[13] and walking towards an end.[14] In my migrant eyes, the church is called to live in in-between spaces. And I caution you from idealising any of these images. They are not to be understood lightly because there is nothing romantic about living in between, being a pilgrim and walking towards an end. If you ask any migrant, they will tell you the pains of journeying in the new land often loaded with frustration, anger, deep sadness, and confusion. Think about the people of God in the wilderness, they complained, got it wrong, wanted to go back to the Empire.

This is not an easy path, but we do not go alone. In the book of Exodus, the people of God are reminded again and again that it is God who has freed them from slavery, who is journeying with them, holding them in steadfast love and feeding them with manna. Once the slaves of Egypt were liberated from the Empire, they forged a new identity, an identity as people of God. In our

---

13 BOU, 3.
14 BOU, 18.

journey, it is Christ who "feeds the Church" so that "we may not lose the way" (BOU, 3). We are not called to be a "wandering or meandering people."[15] Our final goal is set, and we know where we are heading. We are called to be the pilgrim people of God. We are called not just to a journey, but towards a journey *with* God. And maybe we should travel lightly so that we may move easily without being burdened by possessions.[16]

In the new normal, as we merge from lockdowns, we are asked to move forward but as a church, our movement is a bit different because we walk towards an end. An end that brings new life, new beginning, a new heaven and earth. According to the *Basis*, "the Uniting Church affirms that it belongs to the people of God on the way to the promised end" (BOU, 18). We are a church on a journey towards an end. This is something we do not control nor foresee; we live "between the time of Christ's death and resurrection and the final consummation of all things which Christ will bring" (BOU, 3).

As a church, we continuously seek renewal and reform through the Word and Spirit, with Christ the living Head of the Church. We journey together totally dependent on the Triune God to go with us because without God our journey is worthless. We are to follow the crucified and risen one, and our destination is towards an end where the kin(g)dom of God has come. We are to follow as the pilgrim people of God towards an end, to live in-between the world and the world to come. We are to live in the world but not of the world. And for a non-white migrant like me being a pilgrim and to live in between, is to shuffle along the margins, away from the centre. Moving away from the ways of the world – hierarchy,

---

15  Uniting Church in Australia, *The status, authority and role of the Basis of Union within the Uniting Church in Australia*, A discussion paper issued be the Assembly, 1996, 12.

16  Andrew Dutney, "A Fellowship of Reconciliation: A Pilgrim People," Speech, Opening Worship of 2013 Synod of NSW-ACT, Sydney, 2013, last modified April 16, 2013, https://andrewfdutney.com/2013/04/16/a-fellowship-of -reconciliation-a-pilgrim-people/

patriarchy, racism, ageism, violence, and colonisation – things that divide and take hold of us. When we leave the centre, we can actually gain a better perspective of the centre and offer a different view. We are called to a different way of living. In this marginal space we can offer a different language from what is proclaimed from the centre of the world.

Our call is not to be at the centre but at the end, at the margins. Not to dominate and build an empire, but to be a foretaste of that coming reconciliation and renewal for the whole creation, and to point to Jesus, the beginning of a new creation of a new humanity. As a church we are called "to serve that end ... always on the way towards a promised goal" (BOU, 3). To become part of the kin(g)dom to come. We are to become the Church perched on the margins "to be the disciples of a crucified Lord" and "in his own strange way [Christ] constitutes, rules and renews [us] as his Church" (BOU, 4).

## So who are we and where are we going?

"We are the Uniting Church" is the first thing you notice when you open the Assembly website of the Uniting Church. Under this banner you see different images rotating – showing diverse people within the life of the UCA – in congregations, gatherings, protest, singing and worshipping, breaking bread and praying together, First Peoples and Second Peoples, young and old, diverse genders. The images rotate with the following description translated in multiple languages, "a community of people following Jesus and God's call to live with love grace and hope in the world."[17]

Belonging to the One Holy Catholic and Apostolic church, each of us is called by Christ to be a follower, and the *Basis* expresses in a particular way what that might look like. In this essay I have asked questions and have been happy to leave them unanswered.

---

17 For these themes see the Uniting Church in Australia Assembly website, https://uniting.church/

125

As we seriously ponder what our future looks like, let us remember our story. A story that points to the One crucified and risen – who gives us identity. So, we follow. Committed to serve the world for which Christ died, living in between spaces, perched on the margins, may we faithfully walk towards a promised end as pilgrim people of God.

# 10

# The Role of the Tongan National Conference in relation to the *Basis of Union*

Jason Kioa

## The *Basis of Union* and how the Tongan National Conference finds itself in it

On the 50th Anniversary of the *Basis of Union* in the Uniting Church, I present this paper as an acknowledgment of a long journey of struggle to join the Uniting Church by one of its partner churches, the Free Wesleyan Church of Tonga. This paper is also written in the spirit of the acknowledgment that the Tongans have joined with other cultures of the Second Peoples to pay respect to the First Peoples of Australia, past, present and future in commitment to justice and peace.

The *Basis of Union* highlights many years of hard work in bringing together the Methodist, Presbyterian and Congregational denominations. The Uniting Church is ecumenical in its nature and practices. But the idea, which is now a reality, of the Uniting Church being a multicultural church, was not quite envisaged in 1971 when the *Basis of Union* was formalised. At the meeting of its national Assembly in 1985, the Uniting Church declared itself to be a "Multicultural Church" – a great statement and an aspirational one.[1]

But the journey to embodying its reality has been a huge struggle for the Tongan diaspora over the years. It took some years for the Tongans to appreciate the richness of the *Basis of Union*. The main struggle is of course the language. The *Basis of Union* is

1 See WAAMC

written in English and it represents in those eighteen paragraphs many years of theological and biblical reflections by representatives from the three denominations. Although the *Basis of Union* has been translated into Tongan language, it does not reflect the same spirit of ownership and understanding as its English original. It is a mere translation of a finished product of a journey of a mono-cultural language and understanding. I often wonder what might have happened if the journey with the many languages and cultures were captured during the journey before union so that the *Basis of Union* represented the journey of a truly multicultural and intercultural Church, One Body with many languages.

Having said that, I have to acknowledge on the 50th anniversary of the *Basis of Union* that the Tongan National Conference has found its life and existence in the *Basis*. In translating the *Basis of Union* into Tongan, there were challenges. In the Tongan alphabet there are fewer letters than the English alphabet. This means that translation will be more of an interpretation rather than direct word-to-word translation. In effect, translating a word from English into Tongan may be a sentence rather than a single word. However, the eighteen paragraphs of the *Basis* are well explained and easy to be understood in Tongan. The Free Wesleyan Church of Tonga members who come to Australia can choose to find a home in the Uniting Church ecclesiologically, multiculturally, and interculturally. Christ as the Head of the Church provides an embracing platform and more towards fullness when we recognise that the Day of Pentecost experience of many languages is a glimpse of our journey as God's People.

Two years after the declaration of the Uniting Church as a Multicultural Church, the Tongan National Conference was formed in June 1987. It was the first national conference to be established in the UCA and is one of twelve national conferences now found under the umbrella of this ecumenically-inspired church "on the way." The setting up of those conferences was encouraged by the host church but done so in a way that was not covered by its *Constitution*, *Regulations*, or its foundational document, *The Basis of Union*. There is no reference to any, let alone all, such conferences in the polity of the Uniting Church. This neglect is not offset by any of the declarations made by the Uniting Church with regards to its being multicultural (1985)[2] or 'One Body, Many Members' (2012).[3] And yet, all the while since its inception in 1987,[4] the Tongan National Conference has met annually and grown in size to represent the single largest gathering of men, women and children within the Uniting Church outside of a handful of megachurches.

The Tongan National Conference is now a well-established event in the life of the Uniting Church as well as among its Tongan members. It has consolidated its role as a cultural forum and a site for discussions on matters pertaining to the Tongan presence and participation in the life and witness of the host denomination. The mere holding of a conference like this one on an annual basis is a demonstration of the Tongan commitment to the claims the Uniting Church has made of being a church comprising a cultural and linguistic diversity. Since its inception it has set out to reflect on a number of pivotal matters concerning the Tongan identity and its place within the Uniting Church. It has become a significant event. The numbers attending every year is increasing and is a sure sign that the Conference is meeting a cultural need. Its meetings provide opportunities to worship, to have fellowship and to learn and share stories. It provides an event where Tongans across synods can meet and identify themselves with one another.

The Tongan National Conference has, in fact, become one of the largest bodies of people to gather at any one time in one venue in the whole of the Uniting Church. It does so across

---

2 See WAAMC

3 See "One Body, Many Members – Living faith and life cross-culturally," Uniting Church Assembly, May 12, 2022, https://ucaassembly.recollect.net.au/nodes/view/416

4 "Minutes of the 1st Tongan National Gathering in Point Piper," NSW (Mitchell Library Sydney) Uniting Church in Australia records held in the State and Mitchell Libraries.

generations. I have witnessed this for many years as I chaired the Tongan National Conference from 2001–2017. I am therefore reflecting as a participant in the Tongan National Conference but also as an observer. While I have enjoyed the welcome and hospitality received within the Uniting Church, I also experienced as an observer the struggles of being accepted and well understood. I refer to Judith Thompson's model of a progressive theological reflection as I reflect on my experience as Chair but also as an observer over the growth of the conference for many years.[5]

The presenting problem has been identified. The distinction between being a participant and a critical observer has been made and justified. The thick description has provided a specific instance of what happens in the annual gathering while explaining how the Tongan National Conference came into being. It has also put forward the idea that, in its current form, the Tongan National Conference should be seen as an event: it is not a council of the interconciliar Uniting Church. Nor should it be linked in terms of invitations, hospitality, and its bridging function with the Free Wesleyan Methodist Church, or be interpreted as being some form of outreach of that church. The practice of a progressive theological reflection is to propose a theological or biblical response.

One way of exploring what has happened in the life of the Tongan National Conference in ensuing years is to appropriate a contextual metaphor. The most apt is the custom of rolling out the mat, ( *Fofola e fala kae talanga*). This metaphor has been used many times before. The Tongan proverb *Fofola e fala kae talanga* literally means roll out the mat for conversation. Sisilia Tupou-Thomas referred to this proverb in her article on "Telling Tales."[6] In this article Thomas struggles with being Tongan in

---

5 Judith Thompson, with Stephen Pattison and Ross Thompson, SCM *Study Guide to Theological Reflection*, (London: SCM Press, 2008), 21.

6 Sisilia Tupou, "Telling Tales," in *Faith in a Hyphen: cross cultural theologies down under* ed. Clive Pearson with a sub-version by Jione Havea (Adelaide: Open Book, 2004), 3.

Australia coming from an oral culture where story telling is the mode of communication and passing down of traditions. Where there is misunderstanding, the mat is rolled out for conversation. This is a metaphor of the intentional gathering of the community with a particular set agenda for conversation which will create understanding.

The bringing together of the Tongan people from different parts of Australia into one place is like the weaving of the mat. Once the mat is woven it is ready to be sat on. It is still rough in its initial formation, but the purpose is like the metaphor and symbol of welcoming and being communal. People are gathered to discuss matters that are relevant to the community's life.

Where the *Basis of Union* talks about Councils of the Church, the Tongan National Conference cannot find itself in the language of this important vital document. Nevertheless the Tongan National Conference can still become the mat that often rolls out so that the Tongan diaspora and intercultural community of the Uniting Church can sit down for a great *talanoa* about our life together as Second People and recognising that we, with the First People of the land of Australia, are God's People.

It should come as no surprise that a number of questions have risen to the surface. These include: What is the status of the Tongan National Conference in the life of the church? What is its role? What is its function and its reason for being? These questions — and variations of them — can be read and posed in a number of ways. From the perspective of the denomination the issue that presents itself has to do with how to manage diversity. The levels of cultural and linguistic diversity were not foreseen when the Uniting Church was first established.

From the vantage point of members of the Tongan congregations in the Uniting Church in Australia, the key concern can easily become one of how cultural values and ways of being Christian can be preserved in an otherwise alien setting. For others, the status and role of the Tongan National Conference can become more political. If the denomination as a whole decides upon a course of action which is deemed to be contrary to Tongan cultural practice, might the Tongan National Conference provide a vehicle for dissent? Might it also be argued that the neglect shown by the church organisation to this particular conference — as well as to others — can be interpreted as privilege that must be called to account. I am referring to the neglect in recognising this gathering as an important Council of the Church, rather than just a gathering under a Unit of the Assembly.

These are just several of the possible scenarios that lie beyond the posing of these seemingly innocent questions. How are they then to be addressed? In the past, matters to do with the status and role of national conferences was regularly raised in the multi/cross-cultural reference committees of the Assembly. Those bodies no longer exist: the office of national directors has been abolished in favour of consultants whose brief is less specific than was the case for a succession of national directors to do with cultural diversity and the church. There is now no readily accessible process for these questions to be raised in the councils of the Uniting Church.

There is a remarkable irony to this neglect. It takes several forms. The national conferences are combination of work of individual members of the different national conferences and also the product of the work and commitments of Assembly staff. They flow from the passage of the Assembly's declaration of the Uniting Church, "We Are a Multicultural Church." Their gatherings have been addressed by Executive Secretaries, Presidents, Directors and other staff from the Uniting Church. In the case of the Tongan National Conference, the Principal of United Theological College has been a frequent attender as has been the Synod of New South Wales' multicultural consultant. In other words, the importance of the Tongan National Conference has long been recognised by the institutional church, though it lacks any status in the polity of the church and no longer has the level of reporting to an Assembly committee that it once did.

In order to capture better this irony it is helpful to take a closer look at the very first national retreat (as it was then called in 1987) and the annual conference held in the middle of winter in 2016 at the Meroo Convention Centre in the Blue Mountains.

It is very clear that the initiative behind the calling together of Tongan ministers lay with the Assembly, assisted by the Synod of New South Wales-ACT. The first gathering took place in June 1987. The organising genius lay with two well-placed Assembly staff members: the Rev Dr John Brown, Secretary of the Commission of National Mission and Evangelism, and Seongja Yoo, Secretary for Ethnic Affairs. Brown had sent a letter to Tongan ministers enquiring whether they would find "a two-to-three-day retreat helpful."[7] If it were, then the gathering could be organised by the Commission in such a way that it occurred while the President of the Free Wesleyan Church was in the country. A follow-up letter noted that:

> We are aware of some of the pain faced by Tongan people trying to settle in Australia. You leave behind the known culturally and in the Church—and try to relate to a strange new culture and a Church that is related to the Free Wesleyan Church in Tonga and yet is significantly different in some of its practices. This Conference is being organised to help the leaders of Tongan communities in Australia to understand and participate in the Uniting Church in Australia. We will talk together about some of the difficulties that Tongan ministers and Church members face in trying to be part of the Uniting Church. There will be worship services, bible studies, lectures and lots of time to share your own experiences. We have invited the President of the Free Wesleyan Church of Tonga to reflect

---

7 "John Brown to Ministers of Tongan Congregations," 1 February 1987, Mitchell NSW State Library, Ref: UCA National Assembly Catalogue U-1-31 Box 7 MCM Reports.

pastorally for us towards the end of the Conference on the issues that have been raised.[8]

## What is the role and status of the Tongan National Conference?

There are several ways to address this core question. The first lens is through Stuart McMillan's retiring address as President of the Uniting Church in 2018.[9] On this occasion he referred to how the "connection" and "the priority" he had given to the twelve national conferences since the Uniting Church had "shaped and blessed" him. The relationship he had experienced with each one of them had spiritually enlivened him through the triennium. McMillan argued that "the rich linguistic and cultural diversity" of the Church should be seen as "an absolute gift of God." It was his belief that "the Spirit of God is transforming our Church into a truly intercultural fellowship of reconciliation." The church was being "opened" up further to catch a glimpse of "something more of the mystery of God in the process." For this mystery to be realised "[o]ur practices, our theological education, indeed everything about us needs to be reshaped by and through this cultural diversity."[10]

McMillan's reference to "everything about us" is of interest. Should there be further changes to the interconciliar polity of the Uniting Church? A Korean Presbytery had been established on the 11th December 2011 in the Synod of New South Wales-ACT. The *Insights* magazine of the Synod of NSW-ACT quoted the then Moderator Rev Dr Brian Brown declaring that "this is an

---

8  "2nd Letter from John Brown to Tongan Congregations," 11th March 1987, Mitchell NSW State Library, Ref: UCA National Assembly Catalogue U-1-31 Box 7 MCM Reports.

9  Stuart McMillan, "'Hearts on Fire' report to 15th Assembly UCA 2018 - 15th Assembly," accessed December 5, 2018. https://uniting.church/immediate -past-presidents-hearts-on-fire-report-to-15th-assembly-uca-2018/

10  McMillan, "'Hearts on Fire' report to 15th Assembly UCA 2018- 15th Assembly."

important occasion in the life of the Uniting Church."[11] However, the Korean Presbytery was disbanded by a decision of the Synod Standing Committee in October 2021 because of lack of resources and support.

The First Peoples within the church rightly possess a congress for Aboriginal and Torres Strait Islanders. Is it possible to conceive of a structure that bestows more of a role and function on the diverse national conferences than is currently the case? This question needs to be asked now that there is no multi/cross cultural director and reference committee as there once was.

These kinds of questions are not part of the current agenda of the Uniting Church. Its attention lies elsewhere. The fact that the multicultural and intercultural agenda is under the new structure of Circle and Advocate do not provide the platform for broader conversation across the Cultural and Linguistic diversity of the Church. For a church seeking to be one of cultural and linguistic diversity that is, of course, a worry. In the meantime, the role and function of the National Conference needs to be addressed by the Tongan leadership. As it stands the Tongan National Conference is the peak gathering of Tongan-Australians of all ages who are members of the Uniting Church in Australia. The regularity of its annual meetings and its size mean that it is potentially the most powerful Tongan body in the Uniting Church. It possesses social and theological capital beyond any single congregation. It provides a level of voice that cannot be found in any presbytery or congregation. It performs a vital function of worship, fellowship and cultural solidarity while simultaneously creating a forum for intergenerational issues to be named and addressed in a way that could not be done at a local level. The Tongan National Conference possesses a power to inspire and set hearts on fire – but in actual terms of the conciliar make-up of the Uniting Church,

---

11  "Korean Presbytery Inaugurated," *Insights* February 19, 2012, 26, https://www.insights.uca.org.au/features/korean-presbytery-inaugurated-2

its power is indirect and confined to its capacity to influence those who attend.

The case could be made for the Tongan National Conference being something of liquid church after the fashion proposed by Matagi Vilitama for the *Niuean faka fetuiaga*: it is an event with comings and goings.[12] This use of the word "event" is probably rather accurate in its description of what actually happens. Being an event that is regular and expected from one year to another attracts its own form of planning and organisation. It fastens attention on this particular weekend when "the event" happens without necessarily posing or addressing questions to do with "what next." It does not have a formal institutional presence and authority. It is a gathering rather than a council. It is a conference which possesses an executive but lacks the resources at present to be an acknowledged council of the larger church in which it finds itself.

As indicated earlier in the essay, one way of coming at the need for this type of discussion is through the practice of *talanoa* and the associated custom of the rolling out of the mat, (*Fofola e fala kae talanga*). The mat fulfils many functions. It is not hard to see how the mat — and its being rolled out — can become a metaphor for the annual gathering of the Tongan National Conference. There is some merit in thinking of conferences as a semi-institutional form of *talanoa*: where a mat is being rolled out in order to welcome, demonstrate hospitality, engage in worship and share stories and now it acquires a theological purpose. Its most obvious benefit and attraction lies in its cultural grounding.

For the present purpose, the overarching question concerns the status and role of the Tongan National Conference within the Uniting Church. The question of status and role are not exactly the same. It is possible for the Tongan National Conference to fulfil

---

12 Matagi Vilitama, "On Becoming a Liquid Church: Singing the Niuean 'Fetuiaga Kerisiano' on a Distant Shore," Unpublished PhD thesis, Charles Sturt University, 2015, 19–21.

a role of fellowship and support but without having any formally defined status. It is indeed even possible for the Uniting Church to encourage such role and see the worth and value of the Conference, but still not assign it any properly defined status. In matters of status there are varieties of options. There might be, for instance, a formal status conferred upon Tongan National Conference where there is a general disposition of welcome. There might also be a more semi-formal status where the Conference is recognised within a range of national conferences that make occasional reports to Reference Committees of the Assembly, so long as they continue to exist.

One further alternative to this is the current emerging practice. There are no more National Directors in the structure of the Assembly. Since 2018 there are four national consultants who work as a team. The team is establishing a model of "circles" and "advocates" instead of the multicultural unit that the national conferences used to report to. The national conferences now report through the team to the Assembly. It is arguably the case that while this practice will recognise the role of the Tongan National Conference, it is actually weakening the status of the Conference. In a conciliar church what is happening is that the point of contact with the Assembly is moving from a representative committee to a handful of consultants who have multiple other responsibilities.

It seems as if the initiative must still lie with the Tongan National Conference itself. There is much work still to be done across generations, in advocacy as well as in theology. There is work to be done on how the Tongan church envisages its place and role alongside other migrant and minority cultures within the Uniting Church. Is it time for the Tongan National Conference to find a way to support financially the establishment of a position that draws together all the diverse interests and responsibilities it performs. Presbyteries which have fewer members at worship Sunday by Sunday are better staffed than the Tongan National Conference. This step might be a way forward that will enhance the work of the Conference itself and the Uniting Church as a whole.

In conclusion, the 50th anniversary of the *Basis of Union* reminds us of the journey of the pilgrim people whose head is Jesus Christ and that the Holy Spirit leads us and inspires us to work together towards fulfilment of God's will of unity held in diversity. The *Basis of Union* is a living document that inspires the whole people of God to continue to a promised end.

# Conference Reflections

# 11

# Being Guided by the *Basis of Union*

## Andrew Johnson

One of the things I enjoy doing as a hobby is 4D puzzles. They are puzzles of cities of the world. These are puzzles with three layers. First, a base layer of an historical map of the city. This is the hardest and most time-consuming layer as you build the foundation. Then the second layer is a foam map of the present day built over the top. The final layer are 3-D buildings of architectural significance, inserted in the order in which they were built. It represents the three physical dimensions of space and the fourth dimension of time. When I think about how the Uniting Church may be guided by the *Basis of Union*, I think about these puzzles.

Throughout the 1990s, as a Church we engaged in considerable debate about what it meant to "adhere" to the *Basis of Union*.[1] Ultimately, this led to amending the Constitution to say that:

> The Church, affirming that it belongs to the people of God on the way to the promised end, lives and works within the faith and unity of the one holy catholic and apostolic church, guided by its *Basis of Union*.[2]

At first glance, "guided by" seems something looser than the language of "adhering to" the *Basis of Union*. In fact, if you look at the way the *Basis of Union* describes "adherence" in its own terms

---

1 The language of "adhere to the Basis of Union" derives from the *Basis* itself, where, in paragraph 14, the recognition of ministers at the time of union is dependent on such adherence.
2 Constitution, Clause 2 in "Constitution: Basis of Union, Constitution and Regulations 2018," (Sydney: Uniting Church in Australia Assembly, 2018), 43 and Assembly Minute 97.37.01.

there may be less difference than we imagine.[3] On a closer look, however, saying we are "guided by" the *Basis of Union* suggests a more active rather than a static role for this document in our life. If we were to be a pilgrim people then we needed navigational aids, and one of those aids to our pilgrimage is the *Basis of Union*.

If we were to take my 1666 map from my 4D puzzle to London today, I wonder how useful it would be? Some of the big geographical features would be the same – the Thames River would still be pulsing through the city providing its lifeblood. London Bridge would still be there. The topography of the land would be similar. You may find signs which indicate where buildings of significance from 1666 are located. The 400 year old map is still of a recognisable geographical location but it takes some effort to utilise today. So too a 50-year-old document can continue to guide our life together. It takes some effort, and we have built on it, but it still has value if we are prepared to put in the effort. How might it do that? I'd like to offer both some warnings and some ideas.

## Three Warnings

1. We need to avoid projecting onto the *Basis* our own preferred ecclesiology. While *The Faith of the Church*, the first report of the Joint Commission, rejected "ecclesiastical carpentry" as the pathway to creating the Uniting Church, the practice of such "carpentry" has nevertheless been alive and well post union as we've tried to project onto the *Basis of Union* our own preferred beliefs and models of church. Avoiding this trap means the *Basis* should challenge and disturb our own biases rather than confirm them.

2. We need to avoid using the *Basis* as a weapon. It is not a cudgel with which to beat our opponents in an argument. All sides of

---

3 The *Basis* itself claims that "the phrase 'adhere to the Basis of Union' is understood as a willingness to live and work with the faith and unity of the One Holy Catholic and Apostolic Church as that way is described in [the *Basis of Union*]. Such adherence allows for difference of opinion in matters which do not enter in the substance of the faith" (BOU, 14).

many of our debates have been keen to claim their position is "guided by the Basis of Union," however it is sometimes difficult to discern from a reading of the actual document how such claims are in fact true. Just as the *Basis* itself guides us away from proof texting our theologies with the Bible, so too we should not use the *Basis* as a source of proof texts.

3. If we want the church to be guided by the *Basis of Union* we should not rely on lawyers to enforce that. As we grappled with the issue of the status of the *Basis of Union* in the 1990s, at times we resorted to legal arguments.[4] It has become all too common in my experience for lawyers to be asked to resolve theological and ecclesiastical arguments. As a lawyer myself, I can assure you no satisfaction is gained by asking lawyers to resolve theological and ecclesiastical arguments.

## Three Ideas

1. *It is inspired*: If the *Basis of Union* succeeded in bringing the Church into being, does it need to have ongoing relevance in shaping and guiding our life? It has become fashionable to point to its age as a way of undermining its ongoing relevance. However, we continue to find new generations and people new to the Uniting Church who find its contents and vision to be of continuing relevance. This should continue to encourage us to recognise the inspiration of God in its creation through its ongoing ability to inspire.

The documents that sit around the *Basis* ("The Faith of the Church";[5] "The Church, Its Nature, Function and Ordering"[6]) illuminate its ongoing relevance. I have found in reading the documents around the *Basis* that our founders envisaged far

---

4 See Presidential Ruling No. 13, confirmed in Assembly Standing Committee Minute 93.22.1

5 See FOTC.

6 See CNFO.

greater flexibility than we have come to believe through the some of the more narrow interpretations we have come to accept of the *Basis of Union*. So often the apparently novel circumstance we face today were in fact anticipated at the time of the drafting of the *Basis*.

However, when utilising a map now 50 years old we may need relate to the *Basis* differently. We made need to look more closely at the topography of it, the themes that run across it. I wonder whether too often when studying it we look at it *vertically* more than *horizontally*. For example, there has been criticism about a lack of focus on discipleship formation, yet the paragraphs on the bible, baptism, creeds, reformation witness, and scholarly interpreters all point to the teaching and formation of all members. Also, our contemporary critical reading need not render it irrelevant but an opportunity to understand it more deeply.

2. *It is incomplete*: As many people have identified over the past 50 years, the document has clear gaps and silences. However, far from this being a new observation, the document itself identifies that it is incomplete. There is a multitude of examples where the document acknowledges it is an unfinished work. For instance, it explicitly calls for further work on union with other churches (paragraph 2), the diaconate (paragraph 14(c)), church institutions (paragraph 15), and the relationship between baptism, confirmation, and holy communion (paragraph 11). Further, we have subsequently built on the *Basis of Union* with other foundational documents which we have adopted as a Church. These documents include: "The Statement to the Nation" (1977); "We are a Multicultural Church" (1985); "The Covenant Statement" (1994); and the "Revised Preamble to the Constitution" (2009).[7]

3. *Navigational aids*: The document itself includes within it aids to navigation. For example, the introductory sentences in paragraph 15 provide us clear guidance to aid discernment:

---

7 See "The Statement to the Nation, 1977" in TFP, 617-618, WAAMC, TCS and RevPreamble.

- Christ alone is supreme in the Church.
- Every council is called to wait upon God's Word, and to obey God's will in the matters allocated to its oversight.
- Each council will recognise the limits of its own authority and give heed to other councils of the Church.
- The goal of discernment is that the whole body of believers may be united by mutual submission in the service of the Gospel.

The *Basis* provides these principles and practices to guide our life together and they should continue to guide our reading of the *Basis* and the ordering of the Church.

The adherence or guidance of the *Basis of Union* has been most strongly debated through the 1990s when debating ordained ministry.[8] At the Sixth Assembly (1991) through the exploration of ministry in the Uniting Church and the renewal of the diaconate, the Assembly adopted a model of one ordination and two accreditations (Minister of the Word and Deacon). Debate and reflection throughout the Church following the Assembly focused on whether the theology of ordination of the decision was faulty. At the Seventh Assembly in 1994, the Assembly heeded the other councils of the Church and moved to the two ordinations we have today. Through that debate the Church found its way to a conclusion, notwithstanding ongoing debates, through the utilisation of the principles and practices outlined in paragraph 15.

It seems to me more than coincidental that the decision on ordained ministry in 1994 came at the same time as the introduction of consensus decision making, which is part of the way we have sought to embody the principles in paragraph 15.[9] When used fully and effectively, consensus processes do provide a vital tool to being guided by the *Basis of Union*.

---

8  "Ordination and Ministry in the Uniting Church" in TFP, 328-399 and Assembly Minutes 94.15 and 94.34.01.
9  Assembly Minute 94.05.06.

## Being Guided Now

We are now wrestling afresh with what it means to be the Uniting Church not in the later part of the 20th Century but coming into the third decade of the 21st Century. My grandfather, who was there in Sydney Town Hall at the inauguration of the Uniting Church, is now well into his 90s. The generation coming into adulthood today encounters many of the debates and controversies of our union as historical controversies from long before they were born. As someone who was brought up with Spot, Possum Magic and the *Basis of Union* as bedtime reading this is a little unsettling.

When I find myself grappling with change through the lens of the *Basis of Union*, I try to think about three things:

1. Is the *Basis of Union* guiding me or am I guiding it?
2. Who am I listening to when discerning how the *Basis of Union* guides our life?
3. Am I being as courageous as our framers and founders who stepped into the unknown to confess the Lord in fresh words and deeds?

I wish and hope I am just as courageous, but I don't know. The *Basis* was a set of fresh words to create and enable fresh deeds. That posture and disposition helps me think about how this 50-year-old document might continue to guide us into the future. Just as map of London is not just a document to be gazed upon as a piece of art, rather it is a tool to guide our exploration of the city, so too the *Basis of Union* is not simply a document to be read and debated, it is a tool to guide our life and actions as a Church.

# 12

# The *Basis of Union* Through Baptist Eyes

Sean Winter

I am grateful for the opportunity to respond to the papers now gathered in this volume. I will confess, however, to feeling somewhat equivocal towards the invitation to do so "through Baptist eyes." It is true: I am a Baptist; invisibly so by virtue of my Christian formation, theological education, and ministry experience up until 2009, and visibly to the extent that I remain a member of a local Baptist church. Yet, my ministry within the Uniting Church in Australia has now entered its fourteenth year, and most of my teaching, preaching, and leadership has been exercised in the UCA in that time. So, if it is true that I have Baptist eyes, it is also true that I have also been wearing UCA glasses for a long time. I firmly believe that in many ways this has helped to correct my vision.

One way in which this correction has taken place for me relates to the *Basis of Union*. Reading the *Basis* was instrumental in my decision in 2008 to apply to serve within the UCA as a theological educator. The very fact of the existence of the *Basis*, as a confessional document that enabled real ecclesiological reformation, struck me then, and continues to impress me, as an extraordinary act of theological courage and faithful witness.

Baptists are fond of imagining that the only things that really count, ecclesiologically speaking, are the early church and the contemporary local church. In such a scheme, the only conversation that seems to matter theologically is the conversation between "us," the church (or more often and more problematically "me," the Christian) and the Bible. In other words, the notion that history, tradition, or texts other than Scripture can and should somehow function as *normative* sources that somehow regulate the life, identity, and practices of the church, is an idea to which Baptists often show naïve and unreflective suspicion.

The *Basis* and some of the things said within it have reminded me of the naivety of that position. Prior to serving within the UCA, I had already realised that my own tradition was far more complicated historically, theologically, and ecclesiologically than the easy Baptist slogans would suggest. I knew, I think, that the life and mission of the church is always mediated through the important work of ongoing theological reflection, confessional articulation, and institutional organisation. One of the real privileges of ministry within the UCA is the opportunity to serve and teach in a church that doesn't pretend that being the church is a simple thing and, at its best, understands that ecclesiology is necessarily *constructed*. As a contemporary confession, intended to reflect Christ's own constitution, rule, and renewal of the church in Australia, the *Basis* bears witness to the messy adventure that is the church's life in the world.

A good part of my scholarly writing has been devoted to helping Baptists and the wider church think about how all of this relates to the task of interpreting the Bible: what do we read the Bible for and how does this affect the way we approach the task of interpretation?[1] It strikes me as I consider the essays in this collection that we might ask the same questions of the *Basis*: what is its purpose? what do we read, and value, and interpret this text for? what does that tell us about the interpretative stance that we should adopt in relation to the *Basis*? Let me state clearly that I am not claiming that the *Basis* has the same normative function in the UCA as Scripture does; a quick glance at Paragraph 5 should put that idea to rest. Yet, just as Scripture takes up its place within the church by virtue of its capacity to bear witness to God's saving, reconciling work in the death and resurrection of Jesus Christ, so

---

1 See, for example, Sean F. Winter. "Persuading Friends: Friendship and Testimony in Baptist Interpretative Communities" in *The "Plainly Revealed" Word of God?: Baptist Hermeneutics in Theory and Practice*. Edited by Simon P. Woodman and Helen Dare. Macon GA: Mercer University Press, 2011, 273–270.

the *Basis* takes its place within the UCA by virtue of its capacity to reflect, at a few steps further removed, the "controlling witness" of Scripture and, thus, to bear witness to the gospel in its own right.

This attempt to describe the *location* of the *Basis* within the UCA, and thus to affirm its importance, is only part of the story, however. We are left with, and the essays in this volume attempt to explore, two further necessary questions: about the *function* of the *Basis* (its role and purpose in the life of the UCA) and our *relationship* with the *Basis* (how we are to regard, engage, and interact with it).

At the risk of downplaying the difficulties involved in such a move, let me suggest that the role and purpose of the *Basis* within the UCA might be seen as something broadly analogous (with every necessary proviso) to the role and purpose of Scripture in the church. Four emphases strike as especially important. First, the *Basis* is capable of ordering the vision and life of the church around those things that are central and crucial to the gospel. In other words, it plays a role in keeping the church *faithful*. Secondly, the *Basis* is capable of providing some sort of criterion for the necessary work of judgment. In other words, it enables us to see where the patterns and structures of our life might be *unfaithful*. Thirdly, the *Basis* is capable of sustaining an ongoing dialogue among those who are gathered into church-community on the "basis" of its confession. In other words, it draws us into *relationships of difference*. Finally, the *Basis* is capable of provoking change and *renewal*. By locating the church "between the time of Christ's death and resurrection and the final consummation of all things which Christ will bring" (BOU, 3), it is a text that reminds the church of the need for constant and genuine reformation.

As is the case with Scripture, the *Basis* does not achieve these aims just by existing, or even by being read, quoted, honoured, or studied. It is capable of playing this normative role only in so far as we enter into an *interpretative* relationship with it. As with any text, the interpreter of the *Basis* is not the passive recipient of some inherent meaning, but an active participant in creating the conditions within which the text retains a capacity to "speak" (again, in ways that oriented to the gospel and controlled by the witness of Scripture). These conditions are created through sustained interpretative engagement with the text of the *Basis*. To use Paul's imagery from 2 Corinthians 3, interpretation is the work that ensures that the "text" does not become a tablet of stone but, instead, a life-giving message.[2] So, having the *Basis* isn't enough. Reciting it isn't sufficient. We are called to undertake the work of interpretation of the *Basis* in order to create answers to the questions: how can the *Basis* keep the UCA faithful? How does the *Basis* reveal those areas of our life that must now come under judgment? How might the *Basis* lead us more deeply into Christ's unity? How could the *Basis* provoke us to genuine reformation and change?

And here I offer an observation about this interpretative posture that I learned in (and about) my own tradition, even as that tradition so often disregards it. Between 1994 and 1999, I was the Minister of Baptist congregation, in the English town of Reading, which was founded in 1640. In many ways, the church had long been the epitome of non-conformist respectability. I confess I relished the irony of preaching in a congregation made up of local business people and town councillors, reminding them that they belonged to a story that began in the midst of religious and political unrest and, ultimately, civil war, violent revolution, and regicide.[3] In short, somewhere in Baptist conviction, written into Baptist history and hermeneutics, is the idea that there is a "time to break down" (Ecclesiastes 3:3, cf. Jeremiah 1:10).

---

2  For further reflections on 2 Corinthians 3 in relation to these hermeneutical questions see Sean F. Winter, "The Letter, The Spirit, and the Letter Again: Reflections on 2 Corinthians 3 and the Work of Biblical Interpretation," in *Re-Membering the Body: The Witness of History, Theology, and the Arts in Honour of Ruth M. B. Gouldbourne*, ed. Anthony R. Cross and Brian Haymes (Eugene OR: Pickwick, 2021), 1–16.

3  For details of Baptist/Separatist involvement in the political turmoil of the 1640s see Stephen Wright, *The Early English Baptists (1603-1649)* (London: Boydell and Brewer, 2006).

More abstractly, the point is that the Baptist story bears witness to an idea that undergirds the very existence of the Protestant tradition, to which the UCA, notwithstanding its ecumenical commitments, belongs: that some established patterns of belief, organisation, or practice might, in light of the demands of the gospel, the witness of Scripture, the church's understanding of the rule of Christ and, yes, even the UCA's engagement with its own *Basis*, need to be not just improved, or adjusted, or affirmed, but *dismantled*.

The possibility of reform in the church is rarely provoked only by the constructive question: "What should we now do?" It is often made possible by the more disturbing, disruptive, even *destructive* question: "What should we no longer do?" 'Normative' texts provoke and provide resources for a community willing to ask both questions and do so at the same time as they themselves are the object of critique. In biblical interpretation we are learning to see the ways in which the gospel to which Scripture directs us also compels us to dismantle some patterns of life and belief to which some biblical texts bear untroubled witness.[4] In the same way, the gospel to which the *Basis* points us might compel us to dismantle some of the assumed, or carefully negotiated, patterns of life and belief that currently lie, apparently undisturbed, in a numbered paragraph, complete with explanatory heading. This is not to negate the normative function of the *Basis* within the UCA. It is to keep it alive.

So, what "Baptist eyes" give me is perhaps an eye for those places in the *Basis* that suggest the need for a little disruption. In that light, the essays in this volume, which are interrogatory and critical in exactly the right ways, are warmly welcome, and remind us of work that remains to be done.

---

4 See, for example, the essays gathered in Monica Jyotsna Melanchthon and Robyn J. Whitaker, eds., *Terror in the Bible: Rhetoric, Gender, Violence*, IVBS 14 (Atlanta: SBL, 2021).

# 13

# The *Basis of Union*: What Next?

Sharon Hollis

One of the things you hear from time to time as you exercise leadership in the Uniting Church is a desire from some people to move on from the *Basis of Union*, to view it simply as an historic document that made union possible but with little or no ongoing relevance or authority.[1] From other people who, while admiring the *Basis of Union*, you hear the view that the time has come for a new document that lays out how we navigate our life as the Uniting Church, and what we will hold in common belief for the next period. They propose something like a *Basis for further journeying*. We heard this view in a question asked at the conference. The questions I was listening for over the course of the day were these: What might the *Basis of Union* offer the Uniting Church going forward? How does it articulate the unique charism of the Uniting Church within the church catholic? What might it say about the contribution the Uniting Church can make to the church in Australia and the work of the reign of God in this time and place?

One of the delights of the conference was the seriousness with which all presenters took the *Basis of Union*. This was evident in the ways they exposed its weaknesses and interrogated them, and in how they explored ways the *Basis of Union* offers theological wisdom that is both grounded in and open to the questions and challenges of the current time.

The opening presentation by Maratja Dhamarrandji introduced us to the Yolŋu concept of *Rom*-guidance. This guidance helps

---

1  For earlier debates about this issue, see Rob Bos, "Revolting Fathers: the 1998 Protest by the Basis of Union's Framers," *Uniting Church Studies* 9, no 1 (2003), 49–64.

us learn how to live together, how to be community together. It guides our behaviour and our belonging. It shapes us. In this way, Maratja Dhamarrandji invites us to think about how the *Basis of Union* is a guide to our life together as the Uniting Church. It can teach us how to be the Uniting Church; it can guide us in how we behave towards God and each other; it can show us how we walk the path of Christian discipleship. Such guidance also teaches us how to say sorry, to acknowledge where we have failed and therefore to act in ways that seek to repent of what we are sorrowful for. We can see a concrete example of this happening with the *Preamble to the Constitution of the Uniting Church* where we say sorry for our past and present.[2] We say sorry for our wilful behaviour and the failure to notice or be aware of knowledge that is outside the frame of reference for the dominant culture.

The panel that offered reflections from members of the multi-cultural church exemplified one way to think about the guidance the *Basis of Union* might offer us: "How do we story the *Basis of Union*?"[3] In other words, what is the actual living of the *Basis of Union* in the life of the church and how do we tell each other this story? If we receive and are guided by the *Basis of Union* this will open us to a spirituality of living, as people guided by the *Basis of Union*. This notion of "storying" the *Basis of Union* has to mean that we face up to the stories, the voices, knowledges and languages that are absent or distorted in the *Basis of Union*. The respective papers from Joy Han and Liam Miller help us to clearly see and hear absences and distortions. They also help us see how we can face honestly these absences and learn to live more faithfully in the spaces and wisdom of the *Basis of Union*.

Joy Han draws our attention to the special relationships that the Uniting Church is to seek with the Churches in Asia and the Pacific (BOU, 2). She points out that the very notion of "Asia

---

2  See RevPreamble.
3  For more details on the panel and its contribution to the conference, see the Introduction to this volume.

and The Pacific" is a Western projection, a way for the West to name a diversity of countries, cultures and languages in ways that nevertheless fail to respect the diversity, knowledges and peoples. Joy's paper compels us to ask a series of questions that invite us into deep reflection, and to a spirituality of honest questioning of the past and present of the *Basis of Union* and the life of the Uniting Church. These challenging questions include:

- Are we enforcing racial boundaries before we seek to overcome them?
- How has this special relationship affected how we attend to the members of the Uniting Church who are of Asian or Pasifika identity?
- How does this special relationship tend to the way we exported our denominational boundaries to Asia and the Pacific?
- What image of the uniting churches did the founders have in mind when they wrote about the special relationships with Asia and the Pacific?
- When we talk about multi culturalism do we think of the fact that Australia was multi-cultural before colonisation?
- Do we attend to the history of extinction of First Nations languages as they seek to keep language alive in National Conferences?

Similarly, Liam Miller asks us to consider the voices and knowledges that were silenced by the *Basis of Union* – Indigenous people, Pasifika faith and theology, and women. To this I would add Asian theology and faith. The theological project of the *Basis of Union* is in one sense Western, male and linear. Both these papers ask us wrestle with these questions, to honestly face our complicity in colonialisation both in the land we call Australia and in our interactions with the countries we desire a special relationship with. Both papers suggest ways to read the tradition of the *Basis of Union* in ways that will not only help us to make space for these questions but also to find ways to re-story our tradition. While using different language both presentations point us the primacy of the agency of God in the life of Christ and the activity of the Spirit throughout the early paragraphs of *Basis of Union*. Christ feeds, commands, addresses, forgives, awakens. It is the agency of God who reconciles all creation and rules history.

Nevertheless, Liam Millar's careful exegesis of the *Basis of Union* helps us be alert the way in which the discussion of Tradition in paragraphs 9 and 10 sees a change in active agent from Christ to the church. This creates space for us to engage in critical conversation with the Tradition in order that we can have the conversations we need to about the silences and absences. This involves looking back on the past honestly and truthfully, attending to suffering in history and on country and looking forward to the promised end when God will heal all things. By being able to examine these things we will find ourselves compelled by God's polyphonic Spirit to seek restoration, which is God's gift to us.

This understanding of the nature of God, the work of the church in response, and the articulation of the absences within the *Basis of Union* suggests to me that the *Basis of Union* continues to guide the life of the Uniting Church in its local, contextual mission. It does this because it guides us in noticing the activity of God in the world which calls us, renews us, and corrects us. It challenges us to receive God's eschatological gift of reconciliation and work for the reconciliation of all things in our ministry and mission. It invites us to have confidence that God continues to work through contemporary thought and the witness of the evangelists, scholars, prophets and martyrs in our communities showing us where God is already at work and inviting us to participate in that work.

Attending to the questions I have noted here will also help us think clearly about the best form of government into the future. They do this because they invite us to look both to the margins and to God's activity in scholarly interpreters in order to seek a form of government that helps us best locate our life and mission in the margins, the gaps, the silences. The question of whether the *Basis of Union* continues to guide us in ways that help us live together is one that will no doubt continue to be discussed and debated within the Uniting Church. Those of us whose life and faith has been nurtured in part by the *Basis of Union* cannot abandon it before we have wrestled with the difficult questions that have been raised in the papers at this conference.

As I listened to these papers, I came to think that before we abandon the idea of being guided by the *Basis of Union* we must have the necessary conversations where we learn to be critical of the language, world view and theology of the *Basis of Union*. We must face the absence of First Nations languages, cultures and knowledges and seek ways to ensure the absences become part of what it means to be guided by the *Basis of Union*. The call to be a pilgrim people means that we must face our omissions, erasures and failures as readily as we celebrate our times of faithfulness and service. Let us keep in mind that our pilgrimage is to the promised goal. This future is not made in our image, not defined by our projections of race or culture, but is the gift of God who addresses and deals with us through the gospel of Jesus Christ and his completed work and who is reconciling all things to Godself (BOU 3, 4).

So before we create another guiding document let us wrestle with the truth of who we are, with what we have done and with how we hope to live in the future in light of the vision of God reconciling and renewing all creation. The push to create another guiding document could be a way to avoid these critical questions that arise for the *Basis of Union* which I don't think we have fully lived into yet.

If we think a time has come to develop a new document, that might, alongside the *Basis of Union*, guide us in how we are to live together, let us ensure that those of us who, like me, are from the dominant culture with its power and influence, aren't the ones entrusted with the task of developing and writing any such guiding document. Let it be written by those who were overlooked, erased and typecast in the *Basis of Union*. Let any such document be multi-lingual, filled with the knowledge and wisdom of First Nations peoples, and the Second peoples who speak many languages and inhabit multiple cultures. Let any such document take seriously the insights of scholarly interpreters, of contemporary thought, and of evangelists, scholars, prophets and martyrs who speak to us from the geography of the margins, where they encounter the God who lives in and for the margins. These are the fresh words and deeds I long for and which the guidance of the *Basis of Union* both envisages and makes possible.

# Postscript

Postscript

# 14

# A Basis for Continuing

## Peter Hobson

## Introduction

According to Davis McCaughey, the *Basis of Union* was not written simply to bring the churches together, but to guide the church, to inform the church, to shape the church. The purpose of the *Basis of Union* was to help the Uniting Church and its members to enter into "a deeper commitment to the faith and worship of the Christian Church in all its fullness."[1] The three uniting churches were coming together to discover and serve Christ anew.

Over the years, the *Basis of Union* has introduced the Uniting Church to a language of faith that is Christocentric and hopeful, and yet flavoured with humility and grace. The *Basis* has also given us a theological grammar that has shaped our liturgy and our preaching, our conversations and our public discourse. On the occasion of the 50th anniversary of the publication of this extraordinary document, I wish to honour the enduring legacy of the *Basis of Union* and its defining qualities by daring to look to the next 50 years to begin imagining the role of the *Basis of Union* in influencing the generations to come.

---

1 Davis McCaughey, "The Formation of the Basis of Union," in *Fresh Words and Deeds: The McCaughey Papers*, ed. Peter Matheson and Christiaan Mostert (Melbourne: David Lovell, 2004), 12. According to McCaughey, the *Basis of Union* was never meant to be some sort of exercise in *ecclesial carpentry*, or *ecclesial anthology*, piecing together complementary characteristics of the Presbyterian, Methodist and Congregational churches in order to prolong their futures. See also discussion about the intention of the Joint Commission on Church Union in *The Status, Authority and Role of the Basis of Union within the Uniting Church in Australia*, a discussion paper issued by the National Assembly, 31 October, 1996, 4-6.

I will do this by suggesting seven commitments that I believe will shape the Uniting Church moving forward. The starting point, however, is the final paragraph of the *Basis*.

> The Uniting Church affirms that it belongs to the people of God on the way to the promised end. The Uniting Church prays that, through the gift of the Spirit, God will constantly correct that which is erroneous in its life, will bring it into deeper unity with other Churches, and will use its worship, witness and service to God's eternal glory through Jesus Christ the Lord. Amen. (BOU, 18)

The Uniting Church thus confesses that it is a work in progress. We believe that God will bring to completion the good work that has already begun. We trust in God for the future that awaits. This means that we should always be an agile community. Simon and Andrew, James and John, would not have followed Jesus very far if they insisted on dragging their boats and their nets behind them (Mark 1:16-20). In essence, we are a movement not a denomination – summoned to the letting go of idols in order to take hold of the new thing God is doing. In truth, we have not always been very good at this. By God's grace we will need to learn to do better.

Let me now turn to seven commitments of the Uniting Church in Australia, each grounded in, but extended from the *Basis*, that I believe provide a compelling basis for our continuing.

## Seven Commitments Towards a Basis for Continuing

Less people per capita attend church today in Australia than at any other time since federation.[2] But we also have more faith traditions, more religions, more spiritual experiences, and more Christian franchises to choose from than ever before. Churches have fewer

---

2  "Religious Affiliation of Australian: Which religions do Australians affiliate with?" NCLS Research, October 2021, http://www.ncls.org.au/articles/religious-affiliation-of-australians/

attendees, but Christians have more options.[3] Why should the Uniting Church be one of them? What are we offering that others don't? What do we provide, how are we defined, why are we still here?

## Continuing the *Basis*'s commitment to Reconciliation: the calling to Covenant with First Peoples

> The Church's call is ... to be a fellowship of reconciliation (BOU, 3)

There is no mention of Indigenous Australians in the *Basis of Union*, but the work of reconciliation is affirmed as central to the life and witness of the church.[4] Since union, the Uniting Church has set aside time to listen to Aboriginal and Torres Strait Islander peoples – and it has also taken time to ignore them. Our journey together has not been easy. There has been much pain. In 1982, five years after union, at Crystal Creek, north of Townsville a 'Black Congress' was initiated – this was the genesis of a "First Peoples Movement" within the Uniting Church.[5]

Much has changed since then. And much has stayed the same.[6] In some notable ways, the Uniting Church has sought to

3  Andrew Trounson, "Losing Our Religion," Pursuit: University of Melbourne, accessed 1 February, 2022. https://pursuit.unimelb.edu.au/articles/losing -our-religion

4  The 4th National Assembly recognised that the establishment of the UAICC was "in keeping with the spirit of the Basis of Union, particularly paragraph 3." See *The Status, Authority and Role of the Basis of Union within the Uniting Church in Australia*, a discussion paper issued by the National Assembly 31 October, 1996, 9.

5  For an account of the Crystal Creek gathering and the emergence of the UAICC, see William W Emilsen, *Charles Harris: A Struggle for Justice* (Unley Mediacom, 2019), 101–118.

6  There have been important landmarks in our reconciliation journey: the formation of the UAICC, an Assembly apology to the Stolen Generations and the adoption of the Revised Preamble to the Constitution. For a summary of these developments

advance the work of reconciliation and covenant with Indigenous Australians. There is still so much more to do.

The Apostle Paul writes in his second epistle to the church in Corinth that the ministry of reconciliation is God's gift to the church (see 2 Corinthians 5:18). We must honour this gift with our actions. The important work of covenanting in this country is not some sort of optional extra for those of us who call ourselves Christians. It is indeed the heart of the gospel – and provides a compelling basis for our continuing.

## Continuing the *Basis*'s commitment to contemporary thought: a calling to post-colonial theologies and ethics

> The Uniting Church lives within a world-wide fellowship of Churches in which it will learn to sharpen its understanding of the will and purpose of God by contact with contemporary thought. Within that fellowship the Uniting Church also stands in relation to contemporary societies in ways which will help it to understand its own nature and mission. (BOU, 11)

Paragraph 11 makes an explicit affirmation of the important work of scholarly interpreters in the life of the church. Such work, however, is never neutral. Knowledge is power. Post-colonial theories, for instance, seek to raise awareness of how this power is often abused. But of course, it doesn't need to be this way. Power

---

see Chris Budden, "The Uniting Aboriginal and Islander Christian Congress" in ed. William W. Emilsen, *An Informed Faith: The Uniting Church at the Beginning of the 21st Century*, (Preston: Mosaic, 2014), 215–238. In 2018 the National Assembly affirmed First Peoples as Sovereign and endorsed the Statement from the Heart. See National Assembly, "UCA Affirms Sovereignty," accessed March 30, 2023, https://uniting.church/uca-affirms-first-peoples -sovereignty/

can also be shared.[7] Historically the Christian Church has all too often aligned itself with the atrocities of colonisation. All too often we Christians have been the abusers; we have caused the trauma. The Uniting Church and its forbears have been part of this history.

A commitment to post-colonial theologies and ethics seeks to recognise this history, calls us to repent, and equips us for the work of reconciliation and restoration, healing and justice that is often needed.[8] The Uniting Church has in part recognised the importance of this work. We have committed ourselves to become a truly multi-cultural church,[9] embracing and empowering our different cultures and languages and traditions, and being enriched by them in the process. It is a compelling basis for our continuing.

## Continuing the *Basis*'s commitment to Baptismal inclusion: a calling to gender and sexual inclusivity

> ... membership is open to all who are baptised into the Holy Catholic Church in the name of the Father and of the Son and of the Holy Spirit (BOU, 12).
>
> The Uniting Church will thereafter provide for the exercise by men and women of the gifts God bestows upon them, and will order its life in response to God's call to enter more fully into mission (BOU, 13).

Of Australia's mainline churches, the Uniting Church has been the most explicit in not linking ordination to a particular gender or sexual identity." We have done so as a consequence of rigorous

---

7 Indeed, the important work of the church in proclaiming the year of the Lord's favour (Luke 4:19) is in part to empower those who have been marginalised, left behind, forgotten, ignored, abused, traumatised – in the hope that there may be healing and justice for all.

8 See for instance, Jione Havea, ed, *Postcolonial Voices Down Under* (Eugene: Pickwick, 2017).

9 National Assembly, *A Church for All God's People*, 11th Assembly, 2006., accessed May 30, 2023, https://assembly.uca.org.au/mcm/resources/assembly -resolutions-and-statements/item/1689-a-church-for-all-god-s-people

biblical scholarship, robust theological debate, and in recognition that the Spirit has bestowed the gifts for ministry on people of diverse genders and sexualities. This work has not been easy. These decisions have brought conflict and pain and division. But they have also brought joy, and liberation, and growth. Many whose gifts might otherwise have been excluded from the ministry and witness of the church have been included in that ministry and witness, and their ministries have been vehicles of faith, hope and love.

Beyond the question of ministry and ordination the Uniting Church resolved in 2018 to allow local congregations and ministers to conduct marriage services of same-gender couples. Although not the first Christian community to do so, it remains the only mainstream denomination which has adopted this practice.[10] Again, this has also been very difficult. Many have felt that the Uniting Church has compromised its place in the one, holy, catholic and apostolic church. Some are disappointed that same-gender marriage is now permitted. Some are disappointed that marriage equality has not been fully embraced by the whole church.

The tensions generated by these decisions have not been internal only. They have provoked criticism from and tensions with other churches, including those with which we have substantial ecumenical relationships. But they are commitments that we have sustained, and our church is all the richer because of them. That they also opened the door of the church and its ministries to those historically excluded is itself a compelling basis for our continuing.

---

10 The Metropolitan Community Church and Quakers have also made this commitment.

## Continuing the Basis's commitment to the renewal of the whole creation: a calling to the environment

> God in Christ has given to all people in the Church the Holy Spirit as a pledge and foretaste of that coming reconciliation and renewal which is the end in view for the whole creation (BOU 3).

Paragraph 3 confesses the Lordship of Christ over all creation. This has obvious implications for our understanding of discipleship, and our responsibilities in relation to stewardship and care of the environment.[11] In one exercise of that responsibility, the Uniting Church has recently committed to reducing its carbon emissions to net zero by 2040.[12] The Uniting Church's witness and commitment to ecological care is a compelling basis for our continuing.

## Continuing the *Basis*'s commitment to going forward together in sole loyalty to Christ: a calling to theological diversity

> The Congregational Union of Australia, the Methodist Church of Australasia and the Presbyterian Church of Australia, in fellowship with the whole Church Catholic, and seeking to bear witness to that unity which is both Christ's gift and will for the Church, hereby enter into union under the name of the Uniting Church in Australia... they declare their readiness to go forward together in sole loyalty to Christ the living Head of the Church; they

---

11 In the Uniting Church's inaugural "Statement to the Nation" we read the following: "We are concerned with the basic human rights of future generations and will urge the wise use of energy, the protection of the environment and the replenishment of the earth's resources for their use and enjoyment." See "Statement to the Nation, 1977," TFP, 618.

12 National Assembly, *National Climate Action Plan*, 2020, accessed May 30, 2023, https://uniting.church/wp-content/uploads/2020/09/Assembly -National-Climate-Action-Plan.pdf

remain open to constant reform under his Word; and they seek a wider unity in the power of the Holy Spirit (BOU, 1).

Reinforcing this summons to "going forward in sole loyalty to Christ" in its first paragraph, the *Basis*, in its fourteenth paragraph also "allows for difference of opinion in matters which do not enter into the substance of the faith." It would be fair to say that in recent times the understanding of what "matters enter into the substance of faith" has been a contested one. But from its beginning the Uniting Church has embraced theological diversity as part of its identity. Any ecclesial enterprise that seeks to bring together Reformed and Evangelical traditions of faith, and thereby hold in tension the divergent doctrines of predestination and prevenient grace, is one that has already decided to live with difference.

In contemporary theological discourse, it is no longer helpful to categorise hermeneutical and doctrinal differences according to simple dichotomies such as Evangelical and Reformed, Conservative and Progressive. Theological diversity is a gift to the church and to the world when we listen to the voice of the other in the hope that we might discover something of God, and of ourselves, that was previously unknown. We need to take our theological conversations more seriously. The Uniting Church has the potential to do this well, because this was how we began. If we can recover this important part of our identity, it provides a compelling basis for our continuing.

## Continuing the *Basis*'s commitment to confess the Lord in fresh words and deeds: a calling to Public Theology and prophetic calling

> The Uniting Church thanks God for the continuing witness and service of evangelist, of scholar, of prophet and of martyr. It prays that it may be ready when occasion demands to confess the Lord in fresh words and deeds (BOU, 11).

The *Basis of Union* calls the church to be at mission in and for the sake of the world, following the example of Christ. And in 1977, in its inaugural *Statement to the Nation* the Uniting Church makes a commitment to public theology that is thoughtful, provocative and prophetic and calls the world to listen, and the church to obey.[13]

With such a public theology pedigree in our founding documents, it could well be argued that perhaps the Uniting Church has lost its way, or certainly its prophetic voice, when it comes to contemporary public discourse. But then again, much has changed in the last 50 years. The last vestiges of Christendom have well and truly gone. Church scandals in relation to the stolen generations, institutional child sexual abuse, and clergy corruption have eroded trust. Some might argue that the church has run out of things to say and that no one is listening anymore. But this is not the case.

The prophetic call always begins with listening. Initiatives such as *The Cooperative in Brisbane*,[14] and the *Centre for Faith and Public Issues* in Parramatta,[15] have given attention to public theology, and raised awareness in and beyond the church. The Uniting Church's ongoing commitment to public theology, and its prophetic calling, is a compelling basis for continuing.

## Continuing the *Basis*'s commitment to the reign of Christ: a calling to Kingdom rather than Empire

> In entering into this union the Churches concerned are mindful that the Church of God is committed to serve the world for which Christ died, and that it awaits with hope the day of the Lord Jesus Christ on which it will be clear

---

13 "Statement to the Nation, 1977," TFP, 617-18.

14 See https://thecooperativehub.com/ an initiative of Wesley Mission Queensland.

15 See https://www.parramattamission.org.au/faith-and-worship/centre-for -faith-and-public-issues/ an initiative of Parramatta Mission.

that the kingdom of this world has become the kingdom of our Lord and of the Christ, who shall reign for ever and ever (BOU, 1).

The Uniting Church is in decline in relation to church attendance.[16] This is not something that we necessarily have to fear. This can also be a gift. We have the opportunity to reimagine a future not defined by empire building – but by kingdom building, by continually recommitting ourselves to a posture of humility and agility and servanthood. Instead of looking for opportunities to validate our own existence and seeking numerical growth as an end in itself, there may still be hope for us.

To this end, the Uniting Church must continue to strive against the seduction of relevance, for the community of God will always be alien to the world we are called to serve and love (see 1 Peter 2:11). Instead, the church must continue to make disciples, actually create more "aliens," rather than populate our pews with the contented and the conforming.

And when the end of the Uniting Church does eventually come, it will be a sad day, filled with nostalgic story-telling and anecdotes of "remember when". And hopefully it will also be a joyous occasion knowing that we have run the race and been faithful to the end. To think the Uniting Church will always be with us is idolatrous. We must not succumb to such a thing.

Christ's church will always be with us. Witnessing to the way of love and justice and peace. The Uniting Church's commitment to this calling, rather than its own future, is surely a compelling basis for its continuing ... for now.

## Conclusion

The *Basis of Union* is a foundational document, but not a creedal one. It is not beyond revision. In 1992, only twenty years after it

---

16  John Sandeman, *Eternity News*, February 1, 2022, https://www.eternitynews. com.au/in-depth/decision-time-for-uniting-church-in-australia/

was first produced, the language of the document was changed to be gender inclusive. This was not mere semantics. It reflected a changed church, and a changed society, and a maturing in the way the church understood its mission in the world. The *Basis of Union* may well be a historic document from 1977, but it is also a living document in the way that it guides our church today. It deserves our study. It still has much to say.

Davis McCaughey, in his farewell speech as the first President of the National Assembly of the Uniting Church in Australia said the following: "[W]e in the Uniting Church in Australia have no identity, no distinctive marks other than belonging with the people of God brought into being by the death and resurrection of Jesus Christ." He went on to say: "We have embarked on a course in which we ask men and women to forget who they are, and chiefly to remember whose we are."[17]

The Uniting Church is a means to an end. We are not there yet. There is still much to do. This is the basis for our continuing. For those of us called to the journey, how blessed we are to share it with one another, and to have Christ our Lord and our brother to show us the way. Amen.

---

17  Davis McCaughey, "Address to the Second Assembly of the Uniting Church, June 1979," in Matheson and Mostert, *Fresh Words and Deeds*, 84.

# Contributors

**Hee Won Chang** is a Korean-woman-migrant-settler living and worshipping on the lands of the Bidjigal and Gadigal Peoples. The many hyphens tell a different story and connections. Passionate about crafting intergenerational space and learning from the First Peoples, she is one of the ministers at Hope Uniting Church in Maroubra.

**Michelle Cook** is originally from Meanjin (Brisbane) and is an ordained deacon in the Uniting Church. She currently serves as Theology and Ministry teacher at Nungalinya College on the lands of the Larrakita people. Previously, she has served in the Presbytery of Tasmania, Western Cape York with Queensland Congress and as a Bush Chaplain based in Weipa with Frontier Services. She holds a PhD in practical theology from the University of Queensland.

**Maratja Dhamarrandji** is a Djambarrpuyŋu Yolŋu elder from Galiwin'ku and is an ordained deacon in the Uniting Church. He has worked for over 30 years as Yolŋu bible translator for the Uniting Church. He is bicultural consultatant, cultural mediator and ARDS translator and interpreter. He is a former chair of Nungalinya College Board and a graduate of Nungalinya College.

**Michael Earl** is a Minister of the Word in the Uniting Church, ordained in 2009. He currently serves as the minister in placement at Bowral-Mittagong congregation on the lands of the Gundungurra people. Michael is especially interested in Reformed/Evangelical theologies of ministry. He is currently completing a PhD on ordination theology, drawing on the theme of trust.

**John A. Evans** holds undergraduate and postgraduate degrees in arts, law and theology. He is a retired Uniting Church Minister of the Word, ordained 1986. He has served in congregational and institutional leadership placements across four Synods. He is a member of the national Uniting/Lutheran Dialogue and lives on the lands of the Wurundjeri Woi Wurrung people.

**Joy Han** lives on Wurundjeri country. She is a panel member for the Assembly's Walking Together as First and Second Peoples Circle of Interest and contributes to the monthly webinar Black Lives Matter and its implications for our Australian context. She will complete her Master of Theological Studies in 2023.

**Peter Hobson** is a Minister of the Word in the Uniting Church and has been serving in full-time ministry in various forms since 1997. In 2014, Peter completed a PhD on hermeneutics, discipleship and narrative theology. Peter is currently in placement as the Superintendent Minister of Wesley Mission Queensland. He lives on the lands of the Jugerra and Turrbal peoples.

**Sharon Hollis** is the President of the Uniting Church in Australia Assembly. Prior to this her ministry has included serving as Moderator, coordinating Continuing Education for clergy, Safe Church resourcing and as Minister of the Word in two congregations, all in the Victoria/Tasmania Synod. She is a member of the World Council of Churches Central Committee and lives on the land of the Wurundjeri Woi Wurrung people.

**Andrew Johnson** is the Act2 Project Lead with the National Assembly. He previously served on the Assembly Standing Committee for twelve years. He has worked in justice roles with the Church. He has also worked extensively in international development. He has tertiary qualifications in law, science and theology. He lives on the land of the Ngunnawal people.

**'Isileli Jason Kioa** is Minister of the Word at Mascot Wesley Uniting Church in Sydney on the land of the Gadidgal people of the Eora Nation. He holds a DMin and MMin, both from Charles Sturt University. He was ordained in 1990 after completing a Bachelor of Theology and Graduate Diploma in Spiritual

Direction at the Melbourne College of Divinity. He served as Moderator of the Victoria/Tasmania Synod from 2006-2009.

**Ennis Macleod** is a member of Standing Committee of Port Philip East Presbytery and a lay member of St Leonard's, Brighton Beach, in Melbourne. She has tutored theological students for the last 10 years, and completed a Graduate Diploma in Theology at United Theological College in Parramatta and a Graduate Certificate in Divinity at Pilgrim Theological College in Melbourne. Ennis lives on the lands of the Bunurong Peoples.

**Liam Miller** is a Minister of the Word in the Uniting Church currently in placement on the lands of the Gayamaygal people. He is a PhD candidate and an Adjunct Associate Lecturer with Charles Sturt University. His work has been published in Black Theology, Studies in World Christianity, and Colloquium.

**Ken Sumner** is a Ngarrindjeri Korni (man) from the southeast of South Australia. An ordained Minister in the UCA, he currently serves as Supply State Development Officer for the Uniting Aboriginal & Islander Christian Congress-SA. His many previous roles include National Director of the National Aboriginal & Torres Strait Islander Ecumenical Commission for the National Council of Churches in Australia and National Chairperson of the UAICC. He is a skilled public speaker and thoughtful theologian.

**Geoff Thompson** teaches systematic theology at Pilgrim Theological College, located on the lands of the Wurundjeri Woi Wurrung people. He has previously served in congregational ministry in suburban Melbourne and on the faculty of Trinity Theological College, Brisbane. He has published widely on the theology of the Uniting Church.

**Sean Winter** is Principal at Pilgrim Theological College and an Associate Professor at the University of Divinity. Ordained as a Baptist, Sean has been working in teaching and formation in the Uniting Church since 2009. His research focuses on the interpretation of the Pauline letters and theological hermeneutics. He lives on the lands of the Wurundjeri Woi Wurrung peoples.

**Ji Zhang** is a Uniting Church minister who lives on the land of the Boonwurrung People. Previously, Ji was the Theologian-in-Residence of the National Assembly, working in collaboration with Assembly, UnitingCare, and UnitingWorld. Ji was born in Shanghai and studied theology in Melbourne and Boston. His research area is Christianity in China during the 7th century.